Decorating With Plants

Other Publications:

THE SEAFARERS

THE ENCYCLOPEDIA OF COLLECTIBLES

WORLD WAR II

THE GREAT CITIES

HOME REPAIR AND IMPROVEMENT

THE WORLD'S WILD PLACES

THE TIME-LIFE LIBRARY OF BOATING

HUMAN BEHAVIOR

THE ART OF SEWING

THE OLD WEST

THE EMERGENCE OF MAN

THE AMERICAN WILDERNESS

LIFE LIBRARY OF PHOTOGRAPHY

THIS FABULOUS CENTURY

FOODS OF THE WORLD

TIME-LIFE LIBRARY OF AMERICA

TIME-LIFE LIBRARY OF ART

GREAT AGES OF MAN

LIFE SCIENCE LIBRARY

THE LIFE HISTORY OF THE UNITED STATES

TIME READING PROGRAM

LIFE NATURE LIBRARY

LIFE WORLD LIBRARY

FAMILY LIBRARY:
    HOW THINGS WORK IN YOUR HOME
    THE TIME-LIFE BOOK OF THE FAMILY CAR
    THE TIME-LIFE FAMILY LEGAL GUIDE
    THE TIME-LIFE BOOK OF FAMILY FINANCE

Decorating With Plants

by

OLIVER E. ALLEN

and

the Editors of TIME-LIFE BOOKS

TIME-LIFE BOOKS, ALEXANDRIA, VIRGINIA

Time-Life Books Inc.
is a wholly owned subsidiary of
TIME INCORPORATED

FOUNDER: Henry R. Luce 1898-1967

Editor-in-Chief: Hedley Donovan
Chairman of the Board: Andrew Heiskell
President: James R. Shepley
Vice Chairman: Roy E. Larsen
Corporate Editors: Ralph Graves, Henry Anatole Grunwald

TIME-LIFE BOOKS INC.

MANAGING EDITOR: Jerry Korn
Executive Editor: David Maness
Assistant Managing Editors: Dale M. Brown, Martin Mann,
John Paul Porter
Art Director: Tom Suzuki
Chief of Research: David L. Harrison
Director of Photography: Robert G. Mason
Planning Director: Philip W. Payne (acting)
Senior Text Editor: Diana Hirsh
Assistant Art Director: Arnold C. Holeywell
Assistant Chief of Research: Carolyn L. Sackett

CHAIRMAN: Joan D. Manley
President: John D. McSweeney
Executive Vice Presidents: Carl G. Jaeger (U.S. and
Canada), David J. Walsh (International)
Vice President and Secretary: Paul R. Stewart
Treasurer and General Manager: John Steven Maxwell
Business Manager: Peter G. Barnes
Sales Director: John L. Canova
Public Relations Director: Nicholas Benton
Personnel Director: Beatrice T. Dobie
Production Director: Herbert Sorkin
Consumer Affairs Director: Carol Flaumenhaft

THE TIME-LIFE ENCYCLOPEDIA OF GARDENING
EDITORIAL STAFF FOR DECORATING WITH PLANTS:
EDITOR: Robert M. Jones
Assistant Editor: Sarah Bennett Brash
Text Editors: Bonnie Bohling Kreitler, Bob Menaker
Picture Editors: Jane Jordan, Neil Kagan
Designer: Albert Sherman
Staff Writers: Gus Hedberg, Reiko Uyeshima
Researchers: Marilyn Murphy, Heather Sandifer,
Susan Schneider
Art Assistant: Edwina C. Smith
Editorial Assistants: Kristin Baker, Maria Zacharias

EDITORIAL PRODUCTION
Production Editor: Douglas B. Graham
Operations Manager: Gennaro C. Esposito
Assistant Production Editor: Feliciano Madrid
Quality Control: Robert L. Young (director),
James J. Cox (assistant), Michael G. Wight (associate)
Art Coordinator: Anne B. Landry
Copy Staff: Susan B. Galloway (chief), Tonna Gibert,
Elizabeth Graham, Florence Keith, Celia Beattie
Picture Department: Dolores A. Littles, Barbara S. Simon

CORRESPONDENTS: Elisabeth Kraemer (Bonn); Margot
Hapgood, Dorothy Bacon (London); Susan Jonas, Lucy T.
Voulgaris (New York); Maria Vincenza Aloisi, Josephine du
Brusle (Paris); Ann Natanson (Rome). Valuable assistance
was also provided by: Janet Huseby (Berkeley); Jane Rieker
(Boynton Beach, Fla.); Barbara Marsh (Chicago); Janny
Hovinga (Hilversum, Netherlands); Diane Asselin (Los
Angeles); Carolyn T. Chubet, Miriam Hsia (New York);
Sandra Hinson (Orlando); Beth Cocanougher (Scottsdale,
Ariz.); Yasuko Kawaguchi (Tokyo); Traudel Lessing
(Vienna). The editors are indebted to Linda Tokarz
Anzelmo, Jane Colihan, Jane Opper, Maggie Oster, Don
Robertson, Karen Solit and Lyn Stallworth for their help
with this book.

THE AUTHOR: Oliver E. Allen was for many years on the staff of LIFE magazine and TIME-LIFE BOOKS. He served as editor of the LIFE World Library and the TIME-LIFE Library of America, and as editorial Planning Director of TIME-LIFE BOOKS.

CONSULTANTS: James Underwood Crockett, author of 13 of the volumes in the Encyclopedia, co-author of two additional volumes and consultant on other books in the series, has been a lover of the earth and its good things since his boyhood on a Massachusetts fruit farm. He was graduated from the Stockbridge School of Agriculture at the University of Massachusetts and has worked ever since in horticulture. A perennial contributor to leading gardening magazines, he also writes a monthly bulletin, "Flowery Talks," that is widely distributed through retail florists. His television program, *Crockett's Victory Garden,* shown all over the United States, is constantly winning new converts to the Crockett approach to growing things. Mattie Lee Horton is a lecturer and demonstrator of flower arranging. Marvin Olinsky is Assistant Director of Horticulture at the New York Botanical Garden, New York City. Emily Malino, columnist and author, is an interior designer. Dorothy Temple, a floral decorator, has been chairman of the American Academy of Florists; she has planned and executed decorations for state dinners at the White House during the Ford and Carter administrations. Linda Trinkle Wolf is a horticultural interior designer. Dr. John A. Wott of the Extension Horticulture Department, Purdue University, is a horticulturist who specializes in house plants.

THE COVER: A prismatic exuberance of color and a variety of shapes harmonize in a formal yet lush arrangement. Crowning the bouquet is a fragile lavender freesia, while velvet-red dahlias anchor the lower curves. Thrusting yellow-banded tulips and yellow snapdragons counterpoint the rounded forms of orange roses, ruffled marigolds, and red-and-white dahlias. Sprigs of lavender ageratums add a feathery touch to the top of the bouquet.

CONTENTS

Brightening your home with plants and flowers

On a recent cold and windy winter morning, the dining room of a suburban New York home was alive with greenery. On the sill of a bay window was a group of red-blossoming kalanchoes. Suspended above them at various heights were a staghorn fern, some ivies, a lipstick plant and several multihued Rieger begonias. A magnificent fig tree on the floor completed the picture—creating a warm, vivid world that could have been thousands of miles from New York.

"I'm sorry you couldn't see it at night," the owner remarked to a visitor. "With the lights on around the plants, it's breathtaking."

As anyone who has worked with plants can tell you, there is something exhilarating about plants presented with imagination, whether the arrangement is an opulent window display or a simple bouquet of golden daffodils on a dining-room table. And you can do more with plants and flowers than add a splash of color or fill an awkward space. You can use them to frame a view or obliterate it, provide a focal point in a helter-skelter room, soften hard architectural lines, even alter the scale of a room.

To achieve such effects, you need to know just a few basic guidelines. There really are no mysteries to decorating with plants. Designers (some of whom show how they work with plant materials on pages 20-33) usually advise choosing plants and flowers the same way you select a piece of furniture: for color, texture, shape and pattern. Groupings of plant materials selected by these criteria are listed in the encyclopedia (Chapter 5), but as you become familiar with plant materials and with various containers, you will want to experiment. After all, using plants and flowers provides one of the most inexpensive ways to change a room. And, unlike an expensive couch or chair you have grown tired of, you are not stuck with plants if your tastes change or you decide you have made a mistake.

Of the basic design criteria, color is the most obvious because it is so easily perceived, as anyone who has changed a dingy brown den

A fiddle-leaved fig arches dramatically toward a sun-filled skylight. With several other plants, including a large, cascading Boston fern, it is silhouetted against the white background of this dining area.

into a bright family room with a can of yellow paint will tell you. Many homeowners associate plant color only with flowers and tend to overlook the great variety of shades to be found among foliage plants. One family that did not miss those possibilities transformed the living room of their split-level Miami home by filling it solely with tradescantias, whose foliage ranges from green and green-and-white to green-purple and reddish-purple. You can get a similarly colorful effect with the multihued foliage of coleuses or begonias.

MAKING A ROOM BLOOM

The color of blossoms, on flowering plants or on cut flowers, must be considered from a different point of view. With blossoms you are concerned not with subtle shades of greenery but with isolated, often bold splashes of color: an arrangement of yellow roses, a gardenia tree blooming white, a bank of flamboyant pink cyclamens. Your choice of colors may be influenced by a painting or by a favorite rug. Then there is the matter of light, which can change the way color appears to you. A pot of pink wax begonias that looked fine under fluorescent light when you bought it at the nursery or plant store may take on a decidedly reddish tinge in bright incandescent light and throw off your decorating plan. But a skillfully placed spot of flower color can make all the other colors in a room seem more harmonious. It can also affect a room's mood: an arrangement of bright yellow and white flowers in a predominantly blue room will introduce a feeling of gaiety and drama, while a bouquet of pale blue and white flowers in the same room will add cool serenity.

It is possible to surround the whole question of color with seemingly endless rules governing what goes with what, and many people take refuge in the color wheel, a circular arrangement of colors that ostensibly shows you how to combine them. The trouble with the color wheel and similar devices is that there are too many exceptions to their rules. For instance, the color wheel may tell you that orange and pink are a less-than-ideal combination, but many gardeners have combined these colors with great success. The best rule is, if you see a color combination that you like, use it.

A GUIDE TO USING COLOR

There are, however, some guidelines that will help you match flower colors with your decorating scheme:

● If a room is neutral in color—if the walls and furnishings are mainly white, gray or brown—any spot color can be used.

● If a room is monochromatic, and its walls and furnishings are a single color, such as red or blue, any flower of the same color is likely to look appropriate. So will a flower of a complementary color: a red flower in a green room or an orange one in a blue room.

● If a room is decorated in several colors, the flowers can repeat any of them. Be wary of introducing a strong additional color, however, or the total effect may be chaotic. In any scheme, it is best to have one dominant color.

● When deciding on the size of an arrangement, remember that a small spot of bright color is equal in importance to a large area of a more subdued color.

Like color, texture is deployed for harmony and for contrast. The way leaves and other parts feel or appear to feel—the feathery look of ferns, the prickly character of cacti, the velvety feeling of African violets, can all affect a room's appearance and atmosphere. If your furniture is sleek and functional, a spiky dracaena will accentuate its lines, while a delicate fern would soften them. Texture also influences the way color is perceived: smooth flowers appear to be brighter because they reflect light; velvety blossoms seem duller because they absorb light.

Size and shape are also important decorating considerations. A room with a cathedral ceiling may be the perfect spot for an imposing sculptural plant (called a specimen if it stands alone); full, bushy plants are good for filling awkward corners because they soften angles; trailing plants are popular for use in windows because they fill the frames.

Yet none of those shapes or sizes will work well unless the plant is in proportion to its surroundings. A tiny potted plant will look lost by itself on a large coffee table in the middle of a large room; a large plant will be out of place in a small room if its shape can be appreciated only from a distance.

When you group plants, you can mix shapes to get a sense of variety and pacing, or you can repeat a basic shape. One New York designer has noted that although sansevieria, which has sharp, horizontally striped leaves, has never seemed attractive to her by itself or with dissimilar plants, seven or eight of them make an impressive grouping.

Generally, the greater the three-dimensional feeling you can achieve, the better a grouping of plants will look. The simplest way to add depth to an arrangement is to position a conspicuous specimen in front or to the side of the other plants. If you have a typically rigid line-up of potted plants on a shelf or window sill, shift a few pots toward the front or rear, and try varying the heights of some with bricks or some other pedestals underneath the pots, placing the tallest plants in the rear.

This technique of varying height and placement is called staging: you are creating a kind of theatrical set. Plant carts, stands and stepladders are useful props, and so is the plant pedestal. Once a fixture in any Victorian home, where it inevitably held a fern, the

TEXTURE, SIZE AND SHAPE

SHAPELY GROUPINGS

9

pedestal is now used by many decorators to help a small plant masquerade as a tall one so it can stand in solitary splendor. Transparent glass or plastic shelves across a window can lend a greenhouse look as well as an illusion of height to plants placed on them. The most dramatic way to achieve height with a small plant, of course, is by hanging it, as discussed in Chapter 4.

You can also enhance a window area—and make a room seem larger—by associating your indoor plants visually with what is growing outside your home. One method is to use related species indoors and out, cacti in the Southwest, for example, or ferns in the Northeast. Or you can create the same effect with look-alikes. One plant enthusiast has placed a potted Norfolk Island pine near a window in her Maine vacation home. Because it resembles the hemlocks in the woods nearby, she says it provides a touch of the countryside, even on frigid days.

MATCHING POT TO PLANT

As you zero in on your decorating scheme, you will find yourself concerned at almost every stage with what kind of containers to use. With so many styles available—Oriental ceramics, handmade clay pots, mirrored metal, transparent plastic, to name but a few—the tasks of matching plant to pot and blending your plants to a particular decorating scheme offer endless choices. A rough clay pot would be out of place amid French Regency furnishings, for example, because its style and material would seem wrong. In that setting a container that blends with the ornate decor, such as a delicate porcelain pot, is much more appropriate. In any decorating scheme, stick to two or three similar styles of containers. Too many variations strike a jarring note in the most harmonious room. It is best to use

(continued on page 14)

A holiday cornucopia

Since ancient times colorful edibles like cranberries, nuts, apples and lemons have been a source of brightness and good cheer during the year's dark months. At harvest time, fruits were massed into lavish displays and at Christmas laced with pine boughs and the glossy green foliage of holly and ivy. Today, come Christmas, the home decorator can easily work within this tradition and have the added advantage of the extensive supplies of produce always available at the supermarket. Grapes, apples, oranges, lemons and pineapples are typically used, but eggplant, avocados, zucchini squash and kumquats are just as good, and rhododendron or magnolia leaves can be substituted for the classic Christmas evergreen branches. Known to some as the Della Robbia style, in honor of the 15th Century Italian artist who embellished his terra-cotta sculpture with ceramic fruit and vegetable motifs, this ancient form of decoration is being rediscovered today as a pleasing counterpoint to the flash and glitter of many modern holiday trappings.

A pine-cone-chip border outlines this fruit-studded doorway display. The magnolia-leaf background is held to a plastic foam backboard with flat-headed roofing nails.

Decking the halls with eggplant

Still-life decoration, ranging from sumptuous multicolored pyramids of fruit and vegetables on the table to a simple sprig of holly tucked into a door knocker, can put a seasonal cheeriness into just about every corner of the house. Internal architectural features, like the staircase on the facing page, often offer graceful lines to be adorned, and these decorations require little more than the fruits and vegetables themselves. Nails or florist's picks will hold the materials fast and, when needed, backboards can be cut out of wood or plastic foam. Additional life can be given to perishables by applying a few coats of clear lacquer before mounting.

A mantel decoration of eggplant, zucchini and assorted fruits set among magnolia leaves and evergreen boughs generates visual warmth above a crackling fire in this Federal parlor. The fruits and vegetables are held together with florist's picks.

Lacquered apples and the traditional symbol of hospitality, a pineapple, sit colorfully in a nest of longleaf pine, Japanese yew and boxwood on the dining table at the boyhood home of Robert E. Lee in Virginia.

The stair railing at the Lee house bristles with magnolia-leaf clusters and varnished apples that are sewn together and held tight with a nylon fishing line, used because it will not mar the woodwork. The leaves, which turn a rich earthy brown as they age, are soaked in water overnight before they are mounted.

colors that will not steal the show from the plants: white, gray, black, gray-green or an earth color like brown or tan.

In selecting a container, you must also take into account which kind is best horticulturally for the plant. There is the ubiquitous clay pot, which can drain into a matching saucer and therefore presents no watering problems. But many decorative containers have no drainage holes; if you want to use them you will have to double pot your plants. To double pot, place a clay or plastic pot with a drainage hole inside the larger decorative container, the bottom of which should be lined with a layer of pebbles. You can then water the plant without worrying about overwetting it.

THE BASICS OF DECORATING

Each room in your home will present special decorating problems and opportunities, regardless of its style, but there are a few points that apply to all rooms:

• Any scheme will hold together better if it has a focal point—one particularly attractive or impressive plant, flower arrangement or group of plants to which all other plant materials are subsidiary.

• If you have a choice between a few large plants or many small ones, organizing a few large ones is much easier, and the results will appear more orderly.

• Use restraint and do not try to do too much all at once. Experiment with a few plants here and there until you strike the right balance. You do not want a plant collection so large that it overwhelms the room, nor do you want plants so crowded they have no place to grow.

Living rooms and dining rooms are the most obvious places for plants and flowers, but an arrangement may be even more effective in an unexpected place. You may want to give an entrance hall a touch of bloom or greenery to welcome visitors. If the hall is dark, you can light up the area with cut flowers or dried flowers. If you use foliage plants, you can set up a shuttle system, keeping one plant on a table in the entrance hall while its twin recuperates in a brighter location; or you can install lighting fixtures that permit you to grow almost anything (page 17).

The bathroom is another spot that is usually overlooked. But who would not welcome a few posies or a small plant that will thrive in high humidity—perhaps on the bathroom countertop?

LIVING SCULPTURES

Your living room is your showplace, though, the place where you want to put your best and brightest plant materials. It is ideal for a large specimen plant, placed as if it were a sculpture or other work of art. One apartment gardener, whose walls are covered with expensive works of art, feels that the most impressive piece displayed in his modern living room is an 8-foot rubber plant—"the cheapest thing in the room."

Plants can solve other problems in a living room, too. An unsightly radiator can serve as the base for a window garden if you place a sheet of asbestos or other insulating material on the radiator cover to protect your plants from the heat. And your fireplace, a warm and inviting spot in winter but a gaping hole the rest of the year, can be turned into an indoor garden. Many householders decorate their hearths in summer with arrangements of dried flowers or of branches of such evergreens as rhododendrons. You can also place foliage plants there temporarily or you can install a fluorescent fixture hidden below the closed damper and keep foliage plants under it. You will have to remember to remove the fixture before you light the fire, however.

The dining room is more of a challenge than a living room since a dining table tends to limit the users' view to the upper half of the room. Small potted plants may become lost unless you have a convenient window sill. Treelike and hanging plants or plants on pedestals are better possibilities for the edges of the room. Convention suggests an arranged centerpiece of cut flowers for the dining table, but do not pass up the opportunity to bring in flowering house plants at the climax of their blooming season. Any centerpiece should be low enough in height so your guests can easily see and talk to one another across the table instead of peering at one another through a wall of foliage.

The kitchen may be the best place in your home for plants. Cabinets and appliances will benefit from the softening effect of greenery, and the whole area is typically light and often humid. While floor plants may get in your way as you move from range to sink to refrigerator, there is no limit to what can be done with window space and with hanging plants. If you are one of those busy cooks who hangs pots and pans from a wrought-iron circle bolted to the ceiling, try hanging a couple of plants from it, too. Ferns and African violets thrive in a kitchen, and be sure not to overlook herbs, available the instant you need them to flavor a meal.

Plants can sometimes be more than a decorative fillip. Many a home is happily equipped with a garden room, a cross between an enclosed sun porch and a greenhouse. In fact, some people refer to them as live-in greenhouses. Almost completely glass-walled and usually fitted with skylights, they are pleasant for people and perfect for plants. One family in the Northeast has equipped their garden room with a center island fitted with storage space and a sink. They handle potting and watering chores for hundreds of plants there, but when they give a party the sink is covered with a piece of slate and the island becomes a bar and buffet table.

SAFE PERCH ON A HOT SPOT

If a radiator has preempted a well-lighted space in front of a window where plants would prosper, make a boxlike wooden cover to fit over the radiator top. Underneath the cover, on top of the radiator, place a piece of fireproof insulating board, ½ inch thick, to block the rising heat. Put a pebble-filled tray atop the cover and set potted plants on the pebbles. Keep the pebbles moist to raise the humidity around the plants, but be sure the water line remains below the bottoms of the containers.

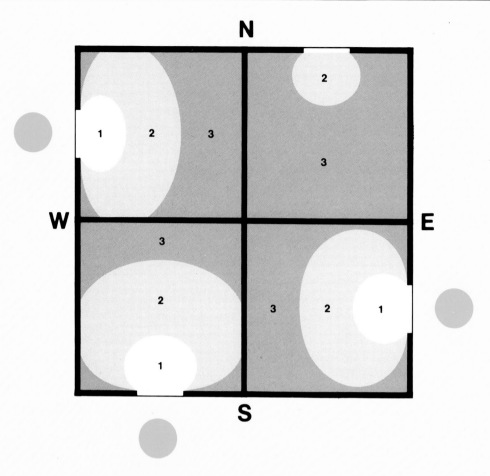

House-plant light from dim to bright

The first step in decorating with house plants, even before you visit a florist's shop, is to analyze the natural light available inside your house. Then you can choose plants that are suited to specific locations.

The intensity of indoor light—and, almost equally important, heat—from the sun depends on a room's orientation, the hour of the day, the season of the year, even the geographical location. Plants in a city apartment may receive 30 per cent less light than those that live in similar rooms of a country house 50 miles away just because air pollutants can absorb that much light. Similarly, dry areas are brighter than humid ones at the same latitude, since water vapor in the air reduces light transmission.

In the rooms diagramed above, Area 1, near east, south and west windows, receives direct sunlight; footcandle readings may range from 1,000 to 8,000 depending on the season. This is the place to put most flowering plants, cacti and foliage plants that need high light intensities. Area 2 receives 500 foot-candles or more; it is hospitable for such plants as rex begonias, dracaenas and palms that thrive in medium to bright indirect light. Area 3 should be reserved for foliage plants, since its low light level—less than 500 footcandles—is not sufficient to bring most flowering house plants into bloom.

Rooms facing east receive direct light from sunrise until nearly midday and are cooler than south or west rooms, since the house absorbs little heat from the morning sun. Most house plants adapt readily to an eastern exposure.

Southern exposures receive the most hours of sunlight each day but show the greatest seasonal variation. When the summer sun is high, for example, direct light strikes only a small area just inside the window; if the roof overhang is wide there may be no direct sunlight at all. In midsummer, even plants that require many hours of light may need to be protected from heat near a south window. Good air circulation helps.

A western exposure is ideal for cacti and other succulents that prosper with a combination of bright direct light and warm temperatures. The slanting rays of the afternoon sun are more intense than those of the morning sun because there is less humidity in the air to block the light. Since the house has had time to absorb heat, plants should be placed 2 or 3 feet away from a western window in summer.

Lowest but most constant in both light intensity and temperature is a northern exposure. The relatively cool, always indirect light satisfies the needs of ferns, spider plants, philodendrons and similar foliage plants that are damaged by exposure to direct sunlight.

These examples of the decorative uses of plants are just a few of the possibilities that await you. Before you proceed, however, take stock of your home. Decorating with plants and flowers, like any adventure into new territory, requires a map of sorts. What kind of rooms and spaces do you have, how much light is there, which way do the windows face? A southern exposure gets the most light (*opposite page*), but for many plants that may be too much of a good thing in summer. At an eastern outlook the light is moderate but more constant through most of the year. A western exposure will do for many plants, providing longer light than one on the east, but the heat of the afternoon sun can harm many species. Even a northern exposure can be a hospitable setting for ferns and other plants that need only a low light level. Measurement of light intensity with a light meter will give you an indication of suitable locations, but the only certain way to find out if a particular plant will survive in a particular spot is to try it there.

SUPPLEMENTING THE SUN

If you depend on natural light, your best growing space is generally limited to a few feet around each window. One way to break through this limitation is to shuttle plants between dark areas and well-lighted ones. This is a considerable chore if you have a lot of plants, though, and it is easier to illuminate plants in dark areas with artificial light.

For plants, the best source of such light is fluorescent lamps. They have disadvantages—they cannot be camouflaged as well as incandescents and you may dislike what they do to colors—but they give off more of the kind of light plants need, they are cooler, and they are more efficient, using less electricity.

Artificial illumination, whether it is fluorescent or incandescent, should bathe the plant with light for 12 to 16 hours a day. It is a good idea to use an automatic timer so the lights will go on and off even when you are away: plants need a regular regimen. You may decide to light your plants from below for dramatic effect, but bear in mind that though illuminating them in this way can produce a spectacular display, it will not be as beneficial for the growth of the plants as overhead light.

TEMPERING THE SUN'S HEAT

Illumination affects temperature. The spaces near windows and window walls are warmed by the sun; in summer, you may need a curtain or slatted blind at south or west windows to prevent plants there from being burned. Most of your plants will not be harmed by cool temperatures near the glass in winter. In fact most plants prefer cooler temperatures than humans do. They also need a higher humidity than most people like—around 50 per cent. The easiest way to provide a comfortable humidity for your plants is with an automatic humidifier, which can be installed in a warm-air furnace or operated as a separate plug-in appliance. They are rather expensive, however. Misting your plants regularly will raise the humidity briefly, but there is little cumulative effect. A better solution is to put the plants into shallow trays containing water that can evaporate constantly: put a layer of pebbles in the trays to lift the pots above the water level. For an added decorative touch, try using marble chips, beach stones or smooth, shiny white or black Japanese stones instead of ordinary pebbles.

Similar in function to moisture trays are planters, which provide the look of an indoor garden bed as they raise the humidity. Planters are shallow boxes that are generally constructed of wood, like window boxes, and made waterproof with a lining of heavy plastic or sheet metal. Pots stand on pebbles inside the planter; if you fill the space around pots with moist sphagnum moss, you will achieve a uniform look and need to water the plants less often. Planters make good room dividers. They can be placed on any kind of shelf or table, or you can build them in permanently.

Another popular method of maintaining the proper humidity combines esthetics with good horticultural practice and is the simplest of all: group your plants. When plants are placed close togeth-

DIRECT AND DIFFUSED SUNLIGHT

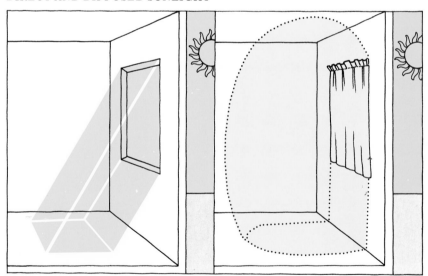

Light coming through a bare window falls most intensely on plants near the glass. Ten feet away the intensity may be 50 per cent less. In summer, when the sun is overhead, the area of direct light is smallest but hottest.

When direct sunlight is too strong and hot for the plants selected, sheer curtains at the window provide some protection. They diffuse light in all directions, lowering the intensity and temperature near the window.

er, they supply moisture to one another, in effect by exhaling water vapor through the process known as transpiration.

Whatever your design scheme, you are the most important element in it, because the result will depend on the kinds of plants you like and the effort you are willing to devote to them. A successful scheme does not have to be grandiose, for in decorating with plants and flowers minimal work often brings maximum results. Moving a plant or two slightly, switching a pot or container, adjusting the light or introducing one additional plant may make a whole room suddenly look better.

If you take the time to become familiar with the wide variety of plant materials available, you will be able to see why, for instance, a podocarpus may be better for your purposes than a monstera because the podocarpus' leaves are slimmer. Or you may choose a jade plant, with its dark, glossy leaves, over a mottled dieffenbachia. One way to learn is to visit friends' homes and see how they use plants. Touring nurseries, plant stores and florists' shops also helps you get a feeling for size, shape, texture and cost. As you explore these worlds, you will get some insight into how to change or enhance your own. And that is the real pleasure of decorating your surroundings with flowers and plants.

REFLECTED AND ABSORBED SUNLIGHT

Walls painted white reflect 80 to 90 per cent of sunlight striking them, thus extending illumination to dark corners of a room. Mirrored walls, especially those opposite a window, are even more efficient as reflectors.

Pale gray, beige or pastel-colored walls absorb more light than white ones, reflecting 50 to 60 per cent of the light that falls on them. Plants placed near a corner benefit from the light reflected from both adjoining walls.

Only 20 to 30 per cent of the light striking a dark-colored drapery or wall is reflected. If you use dark colors extensively, you will need to select plants that can survive in low light, or use supplementary artificial light.

Living designs by experts coast to coast

Back in the halcyon epoch of the very, very rich, Mrs. Astor and Mrs. Vanderbilt could bid squadrons of gardeners to transform a ballroom into a garden with towering potted palms, tubs of delicate camellias blooming out of season, and fragrant banks of gracefully arching roses. Those opulent times are gone. But in their place a new specialty, that of the horticultural designer, has evolved. These experts select and arrange flowers and house plants to add custom-made grace notes to any room.

In most instances, the designers whose work with plants appears on the following pages were retained after the rooms had been decorated. Nevertheless, without the plants the rooms would seem underdressed. Corners would be cold and angular, furniture would seem flat, low and often colorless. The plant designers have added a living element that gives a room zest and makes it inviting.

Moreover, these designers are highly practical. As professionals, they stand behind their work; not only must it please, it must endure. No matter what the budget, they do not recommend certain plants for clients who will not give them proper care. Says Michael Taylor, "A specimen plant may take 15 years to develop, then someone buys it, slams the door, turns up the heat, and the plant is dead within a month. Losing a plant is like losing a friend."

These designers ask themselves the kinds of questions that homeowners choosing decorative plants should be considering: Is there a need for a strong vertical line? Or would a fuller, rounder shape be more appropriate? Would the plants, however beautiful, block an attractive view? Where should lights be placed for the most dramatic effect? Would the cost of a large tree be repaid in design impact? Linda Trinkle Wolf answers the last question: "It is better to have a few large plants than many small ones. If necessary, prop plants up on pedestals so they seem larger."

Those who employ horticultural designers can count on very personal service. On one occasion, Pearl April Richlin made a house call at 10 p.m. to a doctor's home to check on a failing fig tree.

Four tiers of plants are arranged on a French baker's rack against the leaf-patterned wallpaper of an entrance hall. Kalanchoes in a copper pot pick up the color of the rug.

The charm of understatement

Restraint marks the work of Pearl April Richlin, which may seem unusual for a horticultural designer competing with the lush exuberance of plant growth in Southern California. But she has concluded that the houses she works in need little in the way of added drama. Instead, she seasons each decorating scheme with elegant finishing touches, such as the flowering Rieger begonia above at right that calls attention to the coral of the wallpaper while a small Christmas cactus echoes the brighter hue of the carpet.

Richlin believes that containers, especially baskets, can change the look of a plant completely, giving it an individual character. On the baker's rack on the previous page, the containers she selected are as important as the plants. But she frequently masses several plants in one large basket, hiding the pots with ivy or moss, so a sickly plant can easily be removed or replaced but the effect remains that of a single large, thriving plant.

Rounding the corners of a dining room are a pair of weeping fig trees. To add texture without fragmenting the room, the containers holding trees, mums and needlepoint ivy are the same color as the furniture.

Dark green foliage, repeating the color of the cabinet and the borders of the paintings, contrasts with the basic coral motif of this bathroom. At the foot of the bathtub is a laundry basket filled with parlor palms and grape ivy.

Substituting for curtains or draperies at a kitchen window, three pots of flowering kalanchoe, complementing the blue-and-white wallpaper, rest on the sill, while two hanging baskets of grape ivy edge the window.

The impact of massive plants

"I'd rather have an original plant than a reproduction of an artist's work any day," says interior designer Michael Taylor of San Francisco, who champions the use of giant-scaled plants employed boldly as the principal vertical element in a room. Here the plants are indeed a critical part of the decorating scheme, for the room contains no pictures on the walls, no lamps and no window draperies.

Three kinds of foliage plants are used with potted yellow mums in this California living room. At left, a fishtail palm stands beside a primitive mask. Saddle-leaved philodendrons fill the windows, and coconuts sprout on the mantel.

Interiors that echo exteriors

"In my work, I like to do what I call generalizing from nature," says John Voloudakis of Scottsdale, Arizona. "Our part of the country abounds with cacti and succulents, and I like to echo nature and let the world outside flow into a house, using similar kinds of plants that have become adapted to interior conditions." He contends that his plant philosophy would work anywhere: those who live in the Northeast, for example, might grow Norfolk Island pines in tubs to mirror a stand of larger coniferous trees outdoors.

Voloudakis favors cacti and succulents that are gray or blue-green, and his clients welcome these muted notes in their color schemes. He uses these plants where a mass of greenery would be distracting and where he wants strong shapes that can stand alone.

A woolly torch cactus 6 feet tall seems to melt the glass wall with its affinity for the outdoor landscape. The nodes on the ribs will produce salmon-pink blossoms. On the near table is a mammillaria, and at the top of the stairs a branching myrtillocactus subdues the woolly torch's thrust.

Without the lacy structure of this milkbush to soften the curtainless window, this room might seem stark and cold. The plant's pencil-thin branches permit a clear view of the pine and the mountains beyond.

Tropical plants decorate a bathroom looking on Camelback Mountain. With respect for tender skin, there is only one spiky cactus near the tub, the organ pipe on the floor. Softer and more pendulous are a dracaena (left) and a sentry palm (right). On the counter is a milk-striped euphorbia.

Grace notes for landmark houses

John Tilton and Terry Lewis, partners in a Chicago architectural and design firm, consider plants an essential element in their work. "To complete an interior," says Tilton, "we must pay attention to the details, and we feel that plants play a very important role in the finishing and refinement of a well-designed environment. They give a vitality that cannot be achieved with man-made items."

They carry out this concept in their own homes. Tilton's house *(below, right)* was designed in 1909 by Frank Lloyd Wright in his straightforward, angular style called the "prairie school." These houses characteristically have overhanging eaves 4 to 5 feet wide, so the owners are limited to plants that require only low to medium light. A Wright associate, William Drummond, designed the Lewis house *(below and above, right)* in much the same style. Tilton and Lewis both soften their rooms with plants, lighting them from below with canister fixtures that, they say, make the plants glow.

Cascading grape ivy and philodendron grow in water-filled glass globes that hang from the ceiling on transparent nylon fishing line. Heat rising from the two 150-watt canister lamps turns the globes into mobiles that gently revolve. The radiator is a 1913 original.

From the broad leaves of rubber trees to the filmy fronds of a Boston fern, plants create a bridge between indoors and out.

Floor-based illumination highlights a dracaena marginata (left) and a weeping fig (right), casting shadows on walls and ceiling.

Carefully casual bouquets

"Fashions in flower arrangement change," says J. Liddon Pennock, a stalwart of the Philadelphia Flower Show and the Pennsylvania Horticultural Society. "Everything has become looser. Blooms are placed to look as though they are growing naturally. The effect is not studied, controlled or contrived."

Pennock favors tiny bouquets of just a few flowers casually placed in small vases or boxes and pleasingly distributed around a room. These artlessly artful small arrangements may be placed wherever color or freshness is wanted. For example, the little white figure with an armful of cut blossoms above at right brightens a dark corner with no recourse to artificial light.

For a higher arrangement, Pennock often uses a modern version of the 18th Century posy-holder *(below)*. "I call this type of arrangement flowers-in-water," Pennock says. "The lines of blossoms follow the arms of the holder—it is totally without design."

A three-tiered structure called a posy-holder has glass vials on each arm. Dahlias, from pale yellow to deep red, are inserted into the water-filled vials, so short-stemmed flowers can be used to make a tall arrangement.

On a table, a posy stand rising from an iron leopard displays miniature carnations. Vials are placed so the flowers can be seen from above and from the sides. Chilled nightly to 45°, this bouquet lasted three weeks.

A saucy bisque figurine embraces an arrangement of creamy cyclamens and miniature carnations.

Tranquil oasis on Park Avenue

The only deep color in this living room is the green of plants; all the furnishings are in tones of white. "The owners wanted to feel as if they were sitting in a garden," says designer Linda Trinkle Wolf, "but the look had to be one in keeping with the room's sophistication. If I had been aiming for more of a country look, I would have put everything into darker baskets, and added a fig tree."

Tall, airy bamboo palms bracketing vertical blinds promote the illusion of a higher ceiling in this apartment. The descending curve of dieffenbachia (left), spathiphyllum, begonia and bromeliad soften the window view of a large building.

An art that enhances nature 2

An array of flowers casually picked from the garden and held in the hand is a delight. So why not leave it that way, setting the fistful of flowers in a nice container without doing more? Many people do use flowers that way, either because they do not realize that flowers arranged with thought will look even better, or because they associate flower arranging with difficult and esoteric techniques.

With a small expenditure of time and effort, the mechanical techniques of flower arranging *(Chapter 3)* are easily mastered. Combined with a few basic guidelines on balance, scale, rhythm and color *(page 38),* they will enable you to work wonders with what nature has provided.

When you begin arranging flowers, you soon become aware that there are two paths you might follow. One is competition oriented; this world is populated with experts who aim to win awards at flower shows. They abide by strict rules according to the classifications in which they compete. The other path, and the one followed here, is home oriented and is far less rigorous. Its practitioners are interested only in creating something beautiful for their everyday lives or for some special occasion. The home arrangers have no judges to please—only themselves and their friends.

Those who get involved on this private level and who begin experimenting with the effects they can achieve are certain to be more than satisfied. Said one male enthusiast: "You might not expect a guy like me to become so wrapped up in flower arranging. But I find great pleasure in picking up a tiny, perfect flower that is exquisite in itself, then figuring out where to place it to make an arrangement look better. More men ought to try it—and children too. It's a great way to escape from day-to-day worries."

Flower arranging is also an activity that can be enjoyed at any time. If you have a garden, it can provide flowers for the house not only in the spring and summer but well into the autumn. You can

A delicate mix of warm-hued impatiens and gold-heart ivy floats serenely in a trio of china bowls. Such floating bouquets can be prepared in minutes for a centerpiece on a dinner table or to grace a sideboard.

FLEMISH FLAMBOYANCE

continue the display through the winter by buying from a florist or making dried arrangements. If you are an apartment dweller you can have flowers frequently by doing judicious purchasing; a small bouquet or even one perfect flower may be rewarding. If you have house plants, you can supplement them with a flower arrangement.

In flower arranging, the practical and the esthetic are constantly interdependent. This is so at every level of effort and expertise. But you should be sufficiently versed in the basics so you can avoid doing work that appears contrived. A professional arranger remarked that she occasionally gets a request from a local bridge-club member to do a luncheon arrangement. "Don't do anything fancy," the caller invariably says. "Make it look natural—as if I could have done it." This causes the arranger to smile, because she knows that it takes as much judgment and technical skill to create a disarmingly natural and simple arrangement as one much more elaborate.

Flower arranging today is the product of two rich historical streams that came together only in this century—the Western principle of mass and the Oriental principle of line. Decorating with flowers dates back at least to the ancient Egyptians, whose wall paintings and vases frequently depicted the sacred lotus, flower of the goddess Isis. Greek and Roman writers, from Plato to Pliny, tell us that flowers played an important part in daily life. They were mostly used in wreaths and garlands. Darius, the great Persian king of the Fifth Century B.C., reportedly kept 50 garland makers busy; they were the professional flower arrangers of their day.

Greek and Roman mythology abounded in floral symbolism, a tradition that endured as Christianity developed. For example, the rose, earlier a symbol of Venus' romantic love, came to represent the Virgin Mary's pure love. As Western Europe passed from the Dark Ages into the Middle Ages, flowers became increasingly important in religious art. An illiterate peasant of the time could, in effect, read a painting of a woman dressed in blue (the heavenly color) with a vase of lilies (symbolic of purity) as the Annunciation. Indeed, much floral tradition from the Romans through the Renaissance and beyond can be traced through art *(pages 42-55)*.

During the Renaissance, the Italians were famed for their lush gardens, but it was not until the 16th Century that flowers became the subject of complex arranging. Dutch and Flemish masters filled their canvases with flamboyant floral displays, many of them idealized combinations of flowers from different seasons. These perhaps echoed the thoughts of a contemporary historian who wrote, "I consider art wanting and unworthy of praise if it competes with nature and tries only to imitate it but not surpass it." Such painters of floral arrangements as Rubens and Jan Brueghel gave serious consideration to scale, depth and light, qualities now considered fundamental by flower arrangers.

During the same period, the new well-to-do middle classes began filling their homes with lavish and cleverly arranged floral displays, even creating special arrangements for noteworthy occasions. One 17th Century Italian author told not only how to dry flowers but how to make an arrangement with them "to be used in winning the favor of Princes." This type of bountiful floral display has characterized Western flower design for more than 400 years, and the heaped-up mass arrangement is still highly popular.

In the Far East, an entirely different approach developed. The emphasis was not on masses of flowers but on the individual bloom or branch in all its subtlety, and on the special form or shape that it presented or suggested. The idea that "every plant can well express itself" was recorded in 720 A.D. in the *Nihon-shoki,* or *Chronicles of Japan,* and is still the essence of a style that is as philosophical as it is decorative. The results have become known in the West as line arrangements, because they are generally spare enough to show all of each element and are based upon the way each flower originally grew. Here open space becomes just as important as the flowers and branches, and the emphasis on depth means arrangements take on a different aspect with every change in the viewer's position.

The best-known Oriental form is the Japanese Ikebana *(page 78),* which means "making flowers come alive." The practice of making floral offerings to Buddha reached Japan from China in the Sixth Century A.D. The Japanese, with their ancient tradition of nature worship, transformed this practice into an artistic discipline.

The first Japanese to formalize these arrangements were Buddhist priests, encouraged by a powerful 15th Century ruler, Ashikaga Yoshimasa. The early flower arrangements were used to symbolize complex Buddhist philosophy; they decorated cavernous temple halls and reached a height of 40 feet.

In reaction to these extravaganzas, a simple Zen-influenced "low form" evolved. At first there were two elements, one waving toward the guest and a second, more modest in size, toward the host. This floral bridge expressed hope for an amicable encounter.

In succeeding centuries, Japanese flower-arrangement styles reflected the philosophy of the current ruling circle, be it Buddhism, Shintoism or Confucianism. In a 17th Century manifestation, another element was added to the basic two so the arrangement could represent three principles of harmony taught by Confucianism. These three in time came to symbolize heaven (the tallest), man (the

IKEBANA: A GENTLE DISCIPLINE

In feudal Japan, fierce warriors, the samurai, found respite from bloody civil war in the gentle discipline of Ikebana. A samurai would prepare flower arrangements and invite fellow warriors to admire his creations. Shogun Ashikaga Yoshimasa, the most powerful military ruler of the 15th Century, was patron to the masters who codified the rules of Ikebana. This tradition continues in modern Japan: police recruits there study flower arranging with the belief that it will refine their characters and help to counterbalance the brutalizing effects of everyday police work.

THE HARMONY OF THREE

*This 17th Century urn utilized an
ingenious arrangement of hidden
compartments and interior plumbing
that permitted the arrangement of
short-stemmed flowers on all parts
of the container without obscuring its
shape. Each of five tiers was, as the
Latin inscription puts it, "pierced . . . to
receive flowers" and each had a
catch basin to hold water. When the
uppermost basin was filled, water
overflowed through the pipe to the next
level below, and so on until each
of the five basins was full.*

second highest) and earth (the shortest and lowest). This grouping of three elements was so effective esthetically that it came to dominate most modern Ikebana arrangements.

Although Westerners have never adopted the rapt veneration that characterizes Japanese arranging—one American who attended a class in Tokyo recalls that after an hour of discussion, just one branch had been placed—its major ideas are now firmly entrenched in Western practice. In the United States the two great historical traditions, mass displays from Europe and line arrangements from Japan, have met in a style called mass-line that embodies structural precepts of Ikebana but requires many more flowers. In both Japan and the West some modern arrangers concentrate on innovations based more on artistic principles than floral ones: some abstract, free-style arrangements contain no flowers or leaves at all. Some flower shows are dominated by these highly intellectual creations, but most home arrangers are content with less complex designs.

Whatever style you attempt, there are principles from both Eastern and Western practice that will apply to anything you arrange: these are the rules of balance, scale, rhythm and color. Achieving good balance is the most important goal because any arrangement must appear to be stable—even if it is not. Arrangers describe the balance of an arrangement as being symmetrical (or formal) if the sides contain equal elements. An arrangement is asymmetrical and informal if the sides—even though they may actually be unequal—appear to be in balance because of the way the material is presented.

Arrangers can achieve balance by manipulating such elements as color (dark hues carry greater visual weight than light ones), shape (a round flower holds the eye while a spear-shaped one leads it upward), texture and size. Thus a large red rose on one side of an arrangement might balance two or three somewhat smaller pink ones on the other side, even though the pink ones physically weigh more. Arrangers are careful to place the heavier elements toward the center and fairly low to achieve a feeling of stability.

Almost as important as balance is rhythm—the elements of movement in a design and the way this movement leads your eye from one place to another. For example, if you held a bunch of flowers tightly in one hand, they would be jammed together and most would be facing up, with nothing to relieve their sameness. But if you separate them a little to form several groups, then raise a few above the others, your eye will begin to move around the groups.

You can bring rhythm to an arrangement by establishing a progression of blossoms of various sizes, with small ones on top leading down to larger ones; by placing flower colors so that light ones around the perimeter give way gradually to darker ones; by using curved branches and flower stems. If you turn flowers so that some are seen in profile, others are half turned and still others face the viewer, you will avoid a polka-dot monotony. These maneuvers tend to force the eye to move from side to side and up and down over the arrangement. You can also lead the eye from front to back by placing stems and branches so some lean forward and others backward, and by juxtaposing certain colors—cool blues and purples seem to recede, while warm yellows and reds seem to advance.

Perceptual movement of this kind requires that the arrangement have a resting place, the focal point. This point can be a particularly striking flower, a group of flowers or some other feature that is the last, unobstructed element added to the prepared framework. You may, for example, decide to make an arrangement of two or three yellow rose blossoms combined with snapdragons of a similar hue. Florets of the spear-shaped snapdragon, since they vary in size, convey a sense of rhythm and movement, but the full-blown roses, if well placed, add a strong focus for the total design.

PROVIDING A FOCAL POINT

Yet another key consideration is scale. The elements of a flower arrangement should be in pleasing proportion to one another, with none overwhelming the others by being too bold or too large. Often, you can compensate for an out-of-proportion flower by clustering the smaller ones. A violet would hardly be able to compete with an iris for attention, but a hundred violets could hold their own.

The arrangement should also be in scale with its container. A single rose may seem splendid in a small crystal glass but lost in a large ceramic vase. If you are just discovering the world of flower arranging, you may find it convenient to follow the basic Japanese rule that arrangements should be one and a half times as high or as wide as their containers. But do not feel bound by it. As you gain experience, you will discover that thinner, more airy flowers can be taller without any sense of instability. Finally, the arrangement and its container should be in scale with the surroundings. For a grand piano in a room with a high ceiling, you would need a grand arrangement, but on a breakfast tray a small bouquet is sufficient.

Pervading all of these considerations is the question of color. More than anything else it sets the mood of an arrangement, since colors carry strong and familiar connotations: red suggests passion and excitement, white innocence and purity, yellow sunshine and joy. The experts debate color theory and practice endlessly, and it is a key factor in competition judging. But for the home arranger there are no rules that cannot be broken and few guidelines beyond those

WHAT COLORS SUGGEST

set forth in Chapter 1. Combining colors is a totally subjective affair. And the best way for you to judge combinations is simply to hold the flowers in your hand and decide whether you think they go well together and with the room where they will be placed.

How well an arrangement blends with its background is as important as how the colors blend within the arrangement. Aside from the way the colors relate to the whole room, they should complement the table on which they are placed or the wall against which they are set. For example, the flowers in a dining-table centerpiece might pick up a key color in the tablecloth or china. Walls papered with a pattern of several colors are a challenge; try using only one or two of the main colors. Until you have gained experience, it is a good idea to limit yourself to one or two colors, in addition to the green of the foliage. But soon you will want to try an old-fashioned multicolored bouquet of fresh garden flowers in the Dutch-Flemish mode, and—assuming the few basic principles are followed—the result will almost certainly be delightful.

A CHOICE OF SHAPES   If an arrangement has balance, rhythm, a focal point with good scale and proportion, and if its colors work well together, arrangers say it has harmony. The effect it produces, however, will depend on its shape. The most common shape is the familiar round or fanlike bouquet, but there are others *(pages 72-79)*. Triangular shapes include those based on three unequal lines or branches as in Ikebana, the symmetrical A-shape, and various asymmetrical L-shapes and crescents. Horizontal arrangements, low but broad, are used as centerpieces for dining tables or on coffee tables where they will not hinder conversation. Their opposites, vertical compositions that may be 2 or 3 feet tall but less than a foot wide, are good for corners of rooms or for balancing tall objects or pieces of furniture.

A particularly elegant shape is the S-curve, in which the materials describe a gentle curve in one direction above the container rim and a reverse arc below it. Artists have called this shape a Hogarth curve, after the 18th Century English artist William Hogarth, who said the nape of a woman's neck is the "line of beauty" and incorporated that line into many of his works.

You need not adhere to any of these patterns, of course; they are simply forms that many arrangers have found attractive and stimulating. The ones you use will depend on your own need and taste. A pair of crescent arrangements, for example, can be handsome when placed at either end of a mantelpiece or buffet table. You may even want to try a cube-shaped arrangement consisting of nothing but tulips, all the same height, on a square dish. Bouquets and low, horizontal arrangements are made to look equally attractive from any direction; many triangular designs, however, depend for their effect on being seen from only one side.

The shape you devise will also depend on the flowers you have—you may decide that daisies call for a round bouquet. Tall, spiky flowers suggest vertical groupings. Branches with eye-catching shapes may prompt you to try something in the Ikebana manner.

One expert tells students in her flower-arranging classes that constructing an arrangement is "a little bit like constructing a house. You have to build on a strong foundation—and the first thing you build on it is the framework." Elongated materials—tall, spiky flowers such as gladioluses and delphiniums, flowering branches, long greens—are ideal for establishing the basic framework. Big, round flowers such as roses or carnations, or intriguingly shaped blossoms such as lilies, tulips or orchids are added next to form the focal point. Finally, to conceal the holder and stabilize the arrangement, add filler material—inconspicuous flowers and foliage.

With practice, you will be able to create an arrangement to fit any occasion, and chances are you will find working with blossoms and branches so intriguing that the flower-arranging mood will strike you often. For unlike tending a fussy house plant, arranging cut flowers demands but a short-term commitment; it is a means of showing beautiful flowers to their most beautiful advantage.

BUILDING A BOUQUET

Straight from the garden are these kitchen bouquets of parsley, sweet basil, mint and sage (clockwise from front). The aromatic greenery is more than decorative; for as long as it retains its flavor it is conveniently at hand for spicing or garnishing.

The flowering of Western civilization

Though nothing can bring back a faded flower's hour of glory, there is much to remind us of that glory in the historical record left not by gardeners and flower arrangers, but by painters, sculptors and writers. Primitive cave paintings show that early man appreciated flowers for their beauty. And the place of flowers in religious ceremony, from the sacred lotus of the ancient Egyptians to the modern Easter lily, has been secure throughout the history of Western civilization.

The ancient Greeks saw in flowers a way of paying tribute. Countless Greek vase paintings display garlands made to honor returning heroes, victorious athletes and warriors that had fallen in battle. When the Roman Empire was at the height of its power, flowers were used to brighten everyday life: one whole wall in the plush villa of Livia, wife of Caesar Augustus, was painted to portray an elaborate garden.

With the decline of the Roman Empire and the advent of the Dark Ages, fine arts and crafts were neglected almost to the point of obscurity, but they were revived in medieval times as the Church gained power and influence. In the art of the ensuing age of piety, many kinds of flowers were given special religious significance *(page 46),* often perpetuating traditions of the earlier pagan heritage.

But during the 16th Century a new wave of individual expression in the arts challenged the absolute power of the Church. Dutch, Flemish and Italian artists all portrayed flowers simply for their own beauty *(opposite and page 48)* rather than to illustrate a religious belief. This abandonment of strict guidelines resulted in an informality of expression that has endured from the somewhat primitive floral depictions of 19th Century American art to the present day. The basic similarity between the basket of flowers in the Second Century Roman mosaic on page 45 and the floral arrangements painted by modern Impressionists *(pages 54-55)* reveals the consistency with which people throughout history have been fascinated with preserving images of the transitory beauty of flowers.

Capped by a regal crown imperial, Jan Brueghel the Elder's painting, Large Bouquet of Flowers in a Wooden Container, is a garden sampler bristling with blossoms.

Ancient rituals and rites

For anyone who has seen a flower burst into bloom from the mud of early spring, it will not be a surprise that the first civilizations considered them potent symbols. The waterlilies that unfolded on the Nile backwaters were sacred to the goddess Isis and symbols of eternity. The Greeks wove wreaths of laurel for victory and of olive for peace, and the Romans were so infatuated with the damask rose that the decline of their empire is linked with the image of a fading rose.

A mummified Egyptian, flanked by symmetrical bouquets of waterlilies (often called lotus) and papyrus, is prepared for burial in this Egyptian tomb painting of the 14th Century B.C.

A Greek bride (right) is attended by maids who prepare myrtle boughs— sacred to Aphrodite, goddess of love — in tall vases in this decorated terra cotta from the Fifth Century B.C.

A Second Century Roman mosaic includes hyacinths, morning glories, carnations—and tulips, which probably did not reach Europe until much later (they may result from a restoration).

Symbols for a growing faith

When the Germanic tribes of northern and western Europe clashed with the enfeebled Roman Empire during the Fourth and Fifth centuries A.D., the fine arts—painting, literature, music, and probably flower arranging as well—went into eclipse. But as the cultural convulsions that attended Rome's collapse settled, the arts revived, imbued with a new seriousness and dedicated almost exclusively to the celebration of Christian piety. Symbolic flower arrangements often appeared in the paintings of this new age of faith.

Four stalks of lilies, symbols of purity, fan from a gold vase in
Simone Martini's 1333 altarpiece painting of the Annunciation.
The lilies and their position between the Archangel Gabriel
and the Virgin were dictated by artistic convention.

Although intended to be read for its
symbolic meaning, this detail of flowers
from Hugo van der Goes's famous
Portinari Altarpiece (1475 A.D.)
reveals the increasing fascination
with the exact depiction of flowers.

47

Reflections of a rising middle class

During the 16th and 17th centuries, astounding advances in science and geographical exploration began to cast a reassuring light on natural phenomena previously held to be mysteries of a sinful world. In this light the simple, emblematic flowers of the religious paintings of earlier eras migrated to the center of the canvas and were glorified in their own right. The arrangements grew more luxuriant as well, and these paintings became prized possessions of the newly affluent middle classes in Holland and Flanders.

A medley of garden flowers in this still life, *Vase with Flowers*, by Flemish painter Ambrosius Bosschaert, shows the tendency of Post-Renaissance art to glorify nature, bugs included. Such paintings also served as seed catalogues.

The fidelity of Jan van Huysum's *Flowers in a Vase* (1726) marks a peak of technical excellence in flower painting. A move toward naturalism is evident in the asymmetry typical of the High Baroque style.

Cheerful folk influences

However stylized or fashion-dictated one's taste in flowers becomes, the appeal of a simple collection of blossoms displayed in a rudimentary vase remains irresistible. And nowhere is this simplicity more clearly demonstrated than in the primitive and decorative art of 18th and 19th Century America. Quilts, pillows, pottery, wallpaper, furniture and the stiff, two-dimensional scenes of early American folk paintings provide countless representations of cheerful, unsophisticated arrangements of flowers.

Joseph Emery. AGED. 25 & 2 months. 1834. *Sarah Ann Emery.* AGED- 20 years. -1834-

A vase of morning glories, roses and tulips decorates the table between New England newlyweds who face each other in this formal 1834 portrait by Joseph H. Davis.

A flock of birds perches among the flowers in this fanciful detail of an appliquéd linen coverlet, made in New York near the end of the 18th Century. The stem at the left has produced six different kinds of flowers.

An old custom of decorating unused fireplaces with flowers inspired the trompe l'oeil painting on this early-19th Century fireboard. These devices sealed off the fireplaces.

The ornate Victorians

If one period of history could be singled out as the golden age of flower arrangement, it most likely would be the latter half of the 19th Century. For it was then that selecting suitable flowers, treating them, trimming them and choosing just the right vase for them became a popular art that all genteel young women were expected to master. It was also then that the floral centerpiece regularly graced the dining table. In Victorian England, women wore coiffure bouquets so elaborate that glass vials of water had to be hidden in their hair.

In 19th Century America, flower arranging turned to simple designs such as the compact oval bouquets and the hand-held nosegay in this painting of the 1840s by Oliver Tarbell Eddy entitled Children of Israel and Sarah Ann Griffith.

The Victorians deserve their reputation for eclectic ornateness, as is demonstrated by the illustration at left from a catalogue of "masterpieces" displayed at the 1862 International Exhibition in England. Swags, sprays, bunches, tassels and spangles of flowers were precariously arranged in ewers, tazzas, compotes and epergnes, sometimes forming monstrosities. Yet many of these compositions were beautiful, such as the plan for a breakfast table at right from an 1877 book of table decorations by designer John Perkins.

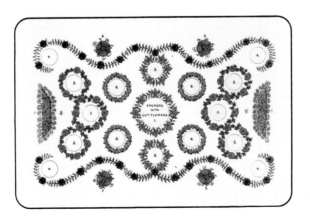

Impressions of delight

Though the Flemish and Dutch masters of the 16th and 17th centuries created a new naturalism in the painting of flowers, it was the Impressionists of the late 19th Century who shed new light on the subject—quite literally. As they discarded the doctrine of exactitude, Degas, Cézanne, Matisse—even the tortured Van Gogh—painted airy works bathed in light and imagination. For them, it was enough to portray a fleeting notion of a vase of blossoms. In doing so, they created a new realm of possibilities for arrangers and artists.

ODILON REDON
Bouquet d'anémones

EDGAR DEGAS
Woman with Chrysanthemums

PAUL CÉZANNE
The Blue Vase

VINCENT VAN GOGH
Sunflowers

VINCENT VAN GOGH
The Irises

VINCENT VAN GOGH
Red and White Carnations

HENRI MATISSE
Poppies

The basics of creating a floral display 3

One weekend at a summer cottage on Long Island, a young gardener decided to put the flower beds in order. One of the casualties of her weeding and trimming was a clump of deep-red impatiens. Instead of discarding it, she cut off the flowers and put them in a black vase, making such a striking arrangement that she could not bear to throw it out when she returned to the city. On her next visit to the cottage, a month later, she expected to find the arrangement shriveled and dead. The flowers had faded, but the foliage looked freshly picked. When she lifted the impatiens out of the vase, she discovered why: each stem had developed long, slender roots.

Most cut flowers will not root as readily as these impatiens, but this gardener's experience demonstrates one thing: most flowers and branches remain alive for some time after they are cut, and some even continue to grow upward for half an inch or more. If they are cut and conditioned skillfully, that extra interval of life can be extended. (A few flowers do not develop further after cutting, among them anthuriums, delphiniums, marigolds, orchids and zinnias.)

The best time to cut most flowers for a fresh arrangement is in early morning or evening, when they are full of moisture; flowers cut when the midday sun is at its peak will quickly wilt because the plant is losing more moisture than it is absorbing. Any flowers that you intend to dry, however, should be cut in the middle of a dry, sunny day, when the plant's moisture content is at its lowest point. Flowers to be used for fresh arrangements should be cut with a clean, sharp knife or butterfly-handled flower-arranging scissors, which have short, very sharp blades; the blade-and-anvil type of garden shears is not recommended because it will crush the stems and block the passage of water—and your goal is to get as much water into the cut flowers as possible.

Flowers that are cut when they are about half open in the garden will become full blown later, so keep in mind how they will

A splash of fresh dahlias accents a fall arrangement of pods, peppers, weeds and gourds secured by wire mesh (foreground). Wilted flowers are easily replaced; the other plant materials will last for weeks.

look in the arrangement rather than in your hand. Some flowers, notably roses and tulips, open so rapidly after they are cut that you may find it necessary to hold the buds closed until you finish your arrangement. To keep a bud closed, wrap it in waxed paper and put the stalk in water in your refrigerator until you are ready to start assembling the arrangement.

CONDITIONING TECHNIQUES   Carry a bucket of warm water (100° to 110°) when you cut flowers from your garden so you can begin conditioning them—helping them to absorb water as quickly as possible—as soon as they are cut. After you have cut the stems, plunge them immediately into the bucket of warm water. Then cut them again under water, at an angle, so that the vessels will not be clogged with air bubbles. Many flower arrangers immerse cut flowers in cold water to freshen them, but actually cold water shocks the plant's system; warm water prevents that shock and is absorbed more quickly. Cut flowers should not be out of water any longer than absolutely necessary. Water not only carries food to a flower's cells, it also swells the cells up like balloons, thus keeping the stem erect. Without water, the flower will droop and quickly die.

Once indoors, stand the flowers in warm water in a cool place for several hours. The combination of warm water around the stems and cooler air around the tops will help the flowers to take on water faster than they lose it. When the stems have filled—the time varies with different species—the flowers are ready for arranging. (If you do not intend to use them within a few hours, a refrigerator is an ideal place to store conditioned flowers: it will keep them fresh and crisp like heads of lettuce.)

Begin your arrangement by cutting the stems, at an angle again, to the length they will have to be. To estimate that length fairly accurately, you can set the container near the edge of your worktable so you can hold each uncut stem beside it. After cutting the stems to the desired length, strip off all the foliage that would be underwater in the arrangement. Foliage will decompose quickly under water, fouling it with harmful bacteria.

STEM TREATMENTS   Pithy stems such as those of some chrysanthemums and stocks should be split vertically an inch or so at the bottom with a sharp knife or razor blade so they will take up water more efficiently. The same technique works well with woody stems, such as rose canes and forsythia branches. Flowers that have milky sap, such as poppies and poinsettias, need to have their stem ends seared; if they are left untreated, the water-absorbing tubes will become clogged with congealed sap. To sear a stem end, hold it for an instant in a cigarette-lighter or gas-burner flame, or pour boiling water over it.

Flowers that grow from bulbs should be cut so there is no vestige of the white section below the soil line, as that portion of the plant will not absorb moisture properly. A few types of flowers and greens—notably violets, lilies of the valley, hydrangeas, ivies and ferns—benefit from being entirely immersed in tepid water for several minutes before the standard conditioning is started.

PRESERVING FRESHNESS

Adding a commercial preservative to the water for the arrangement will help your cut flowers and greens last longer. Such preservatives contain an antibacterial agent as well as nutrients. Start each arrangement in a preservative solution, but thereafter add only untreated fresh water each day. If commercial preservative is not available you can make one; it is not as effective but is better than none at all. Add a teaspoon of household chlorine bleach or one eighth of a tablespoon of borax (either is an antibacterial agent) to a quart of lemon-lime soda (a source of nutritive sucrose). Make sure that any leftover preservative is clearly labeled and stored where it will not be mistaken for a soft drink.

Some flower arrangers believe that a couple of aspirin tablets or copper pennies dropped into the water will prolong the life of cut blossoms. Actually, while neither the pennies nor the aspirin tablets will harm the flowers, neither will they have any beneficial effect.

PROLONGING THE LIFE OF CUT FLOWERS

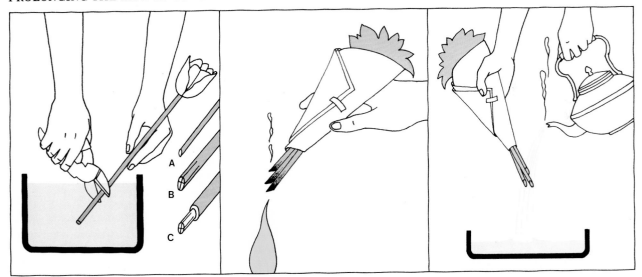

Using flower shears or a knife, trim all stems under water. Cut at a slant for greater water absorption (A). In a woody stem, slice an inch-deep cross (B). If the stem bears flower clusters, scrape off an inch or so of bark (C).

Over a flame, char stems that ooze a milky sap, such as those of dahlias or poppies. Protect flowers with a cone of newspaper. Plunge blackened stem ends into water. Charring keeps sap from blocking water.

Alternatively, pour boiling water over stems oozing milky sap, wrapping the foliage and flowers to shield them from the steam. This method is faster but less effective than charring the stem ends with a flame.

Still other arrangers swear by sugar as an effective preservative. Sugar is a nutrient, of course, but it promotes harmful bacterial growth if it is used alone in the water.

The best way to help cut flowers flourish is to keep their environment spotlessly clean and cool. Before you start an arrangement, make sure the container has been scrubbed free of any debris from the previous bouquet.

THE FLORIST'S WARES
Flowers that are purchased from a florist will almost certainly have been conditioned and can be used immediately in an arrangement. You should take time, however, to recut the ends of the stems under warm water. And check flower freshness even before you buy. The plump calyx just below the petals should be green and fresh looking. Stem cuts should not be blackened. And the flower petals should be crisp and unblemished.

Ask your florist what kinds of flowers he expects to have available in coming weeks. If you want them, he may be able to get unusual varieties for you from his wholesaler. A florist may even be willing to sell you what are known in the trade as "number twos," odd single flowers or blossoms with bent stems that are cheaper than his best wares but just as good for arranging. Discuss foliage greens with him; he may only have a few, such as eucalyptus, lemon, huckleberry or asparagus fern, but he may be able to get pittosporum or camellia leaves for you.

Do not hesitate to buy just a few flowers at a time. One enthusiast has a standing order for three dollars' worth of flowers a week. "One rose costs 50 cents, but you can do a lot with one rose in a bud vase," he says. "In the bedroom, we often have a single gardenia floating in a small dish. Imagine waking in the morning to a whiff of that fragrance."

Special tools and mechanical aids are not usually necessary when you are working with single buds or flowers. But any arrangement that is at all complex is easier to make with aids that are readily available at garden-supply centers and florists' shops. Asymmetrical designs, Ikebana arrangements and horizontal groupings are among the constructions that are virtually impossible to attain without such aids. At a minimum, you will need contrivances to hold plant materials securely in their containers, plus a sharp knife or flower shears, florist's tape and wire.

THE STEMS IMPALED
Of all the devices for holding flower stems and branches in place, the pinholder, which looks like a miniature bed of nails, is probably favored by a majority of experienced arrangers, who feel it permits the most precise placement of plant materials. It consists of a heavy metal block with sharp pins sticking up from it on which plant

materials are impaled. Pinholders are available in several sizes in round, oval and rectangular shapes, and in interlocking types that are handy for some large arrangements. The cupholder, which is a small water-holding receptacle with a pinholder inside, is useful for making an arrangement in a basket or other container that will not hold water or for adding a small number of freshly cut live flowers to a dried setting. A similar mini-aid is the orchid tube, a tiny vial that holds enough water for a single stem; it can be taped or wired to any part of an arrangement to hold a fresh flower.

It is difficult to impale delicate or pulpy stems on a pinholder. You can overcome that problem by tying a short length of a sturdier stem alongside the delicate one with florist's wire or tape and impaling the pair. Sometimes you can insert a stem or florist's wire

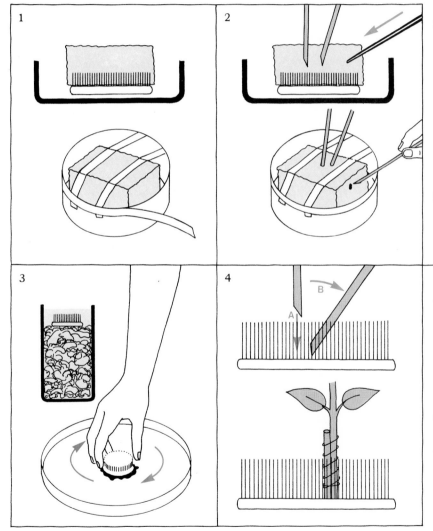

FLORAL UNDERPINNINGS

1. *Floral foam can easily be cut to fit a container of any shape. To place flowers horizontally, let the foam extend about an inch above the rim of the container and, for stability, anchor the foam with a pinholder (top). Alternatively, secure the foam with florist's tape torn in half lengthwise (bottom). Saturate the foam with water. Light-green foam is ready in five minutes; the darker green type may need to soak.*

2. *If a stem is so fragile that it bends, pierce the foam with an awl (top) before you position the flower. Stiff stems cut at an angle can be pushed directly into wet foam (bottom).*

3. *To steady a top-heavy arrangement in a shallow container, use floral clay to fasten a pinholder down. Lay a clay rope under the bottom edge of the pinholder; press down firmly with a twisting motion. In a tall vase, prop up the holder with crumpled newspaper (left).*

4. *To place a flower at an angle in a pinholder, push its stem in vertically (A), then press down at an angle (B) until the desired position is attained. If a stem is too thin to catch on the pins, tie a short piece from another stem to the thin one with florist's wire. Then insert the pair in the pinholder (bottom).*

inside a hollow stem to reinforce it. If a flower is too heavy for a stem impaled at an angle, you can prop it up with another piece of stem placed under the first as a support.

Lightweight pinholders may need to be anchored in the container with waterproof floral clay, which looks like modeling clay and is sold in block form. Before you attach the holder to a container with clay, make sure all three elements are absolutely dry. Break off a small piece of clay and roll it between your palms into a ropelike strip about a quarter of an inch in diameter and long enough to fit around the pinholder. Place the strip of clay in a circle on the bottom edge of the pinholder and press the pinholder firmly onto the container, twisting the holder to distribute the clay evenly *(page 61)*. The clay will keep the holder anchored securely in place, even after you have added water.

Occasionally, you will have to position a pinholder away from the bottom of a container—when the flower stems are too short to reach the bottom of a tall vase, for instance. Fill the container with stones, sand or even crumpled wet newspapers to the desired level, and set the pinholder on the top.

Floral foam, a spongelike plastic that can be cut to any size and shape, is nearly as popular as the pinholder and is easier for

TECHNIQUES FOR SHAPING

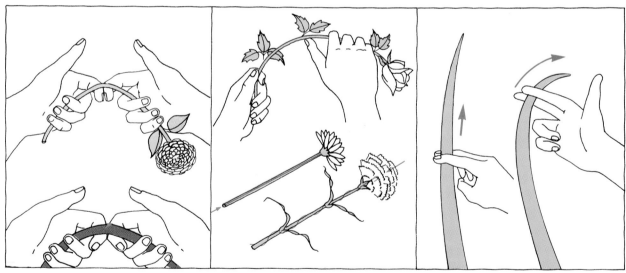

To shape a thin, hard stem or branch, hold it with both hands, forefingers touching (top). Bend downward gently, repeating until the stem holds a curve. Before bending thick branches, slash the upper side of the bend halfway through (bottom).

Grasp a pliable green stem at each end and bend gently several times (top). Before bending a delicate or hollow stem, run a wire through it from bottom to top (center). For a jointed stem, push a wire through the flower and wrap the stem with it (bottom).

To set a curve in a green blade such as that of an iris, wet the blade and grasp it between forefinger and middle finger (left). Slide your fingers up and off the blade several times in an arcing motion, with the underside of the blade inside the arc (right).

beginners to use. It becomes pliable when wet and retains water for several days, though you still must add water periodically. Its main drawback is that it does wear out in time, while a well-made pinholder is indestructible.

Before you insert a stem in a block of floral foam, soak the foam thoroughly. If it is carefully fitted in a narrow container, it will hold most arrangements without additional support. If you need to secure the foam for a top-heavy arrangement in a low container, you can impale it on a pinholder attached with floral clay to the bottom of the container, or you can use half-width strips of waterproof florist's tape to hold the foam, attaching the strips to the edge of the container while both are still dry *(page 61)*.

To insert a stem in wet foam, cut the stem at an angle so it will form a point and push it in. If the stem is fragile or pulpy, make a hole in the foam first with a nail, awl or ice pick. Floral foam is particularly useful in making horizontal arrangements in which flower stems must be held near the rim of the container; the moist foam will keep the flowers from wilting almost as effectively as if they were actually standing in water.

A third device for holding stems, especially convenient for thick, woody branches, is small-mesh chicken wire folded and rolled so it fits snugly in the container. This wire is inexpensive and can be purchased at most hardware stores. It gives flowers the best access to water. Chicken wire should be removed from its container and cleaned each time you change the arrangement, so bits of stem do not promote harmful bacterial growth. The major disadvantage of chicken wire is that it sometimes cuts or bruises tender stems as they are pushed through it.

Florist's wire is useful for fixing parts of an arrangement securely in place, for reinforcing weak stems and for maintaining them in curved or twisted shapes. It is available in green 12- or 18-inch lengths of varying thicknesses. To reinforce a hollow stem with florist's wire, carefully push the wire up inside the stem all the way to the flower head; to strengthen a solid stem, insert the wire down through the center of the flower head and wrap it around the stem several times *(opposite page)*.

Occasionally, you will want to make an artificial stem, either for a flower that has lost its stem or for a flower that is to be dried. To do so, push a length of florist's wire through the center of the flower from below until about an inch of wire protrudes. Bend the tip over to form a hook and gently draw the wire back until the hook is firmly implanted in the blossom and is barely visible. After the flower has been dried, wrap the wire stem with green florist's tape. Artificial

ARRANGEMENTS IN FOAM

ARTIFICIAL STEMS

stems and stems that have been wired can be bent any way you want, perhaps trailing over the edge of the container or sweeping down from it as in an S-shaped arrangement *(pages 76-77)*. Leaves like those of irises and tulips can be curved by wetting them and sliding each between two fingers *(page 62)*. Often simple pruning of a leafy stem will reveal an attractive curve that otherwise would have been hidden by the foliage.

No matter how you plan to shape a branch or stem or leaf, there is a container that will suit your arrangement best, be it a vase, pot, bowl, dish or empty coffee can. Some arrangers own such large collections of containers they have little trouble matching a vase to the height and color of the flowers, but a few basic shapes and sizes will serve most purposes.

There are five basic container shapes that are commonly used in flower arranging:

● The round, globelike bowl with an ample opening on top, useful for circular arrangements and massed bouquets.

● The square or rectangular vase, which works well for almost any style of arrangement, including those with just a few elements.

● The round, narrow-necked vase such as a pitcher or a bottle, which many arrangers prefer for old-fashioned bouquets.

● The tall, tubular vase, good for vertical flower arrangements and for holding branches or dried grasses and fern fronds.

● The low, oblong dish, used for some Ikebana arrangements and for floating single specimen flowers.

You probably will want at least one of each of these types. You may also want to have your favorite shapes in more than one kind of material (and perhaps also in several colors). Ceramic containers are popular because they are usually unobtrusive and do not upstage an arrangement. Glass, although it is often beautiful in itself, may be unsuitable if you want to conceal stems and mechanical supports. Metal containers, especially those that are crafted of silver and brass, are excellent for formal settings. Plastic containers can be surprisingly attractive, especially those that resemble ceramic (they cost a good deal less). Baskets are popular for dried arrangements and, with water-holding containers inside, they can be used for live arrangements, too.

The color of the container contributes to an arrangement's overall effect. Bright hues may introduce a jarring note. Neutral or muted tones, such as gray, white, black or green, and earth colors, such as beige, tan and reddish-brown, are the most adaptable. If you want to use an elegant multicolored container, limit the arrangement to flowers that repeat one of the vase's major colors. A multicolored arrangement in a patterned vase of many colors might produce a distracting crazy-quilt effect.

An inexpensive way to acquire a collection of containers is to make some of them yourself. Look around your house: metal cans, old jars, jugs, glassware, plastic food containers, bottles and all sorts of chinaware are just some of the items that can be painted, stained, covered with lacquered paper or otherwise converted. Some can even be used just as they are. One arranger delighted a hospitalized friend by sending him a small bouquet of flowers set in a beer can, with a note suggesting they get together "to hoist a few" after the friend recovered.

Such a spur-of-the-moment bouquet is one of the delights of flower arranging, but usually you will want to think about several more formal considerations when you are putting an arrangement together. Where will it go? Are the colors appropriate in that place? How large should the arrangement be, and from what angles will it be viewed? What container will serve best? Make a rough sketch of the arrangement you plan, showing where you will place flowers, greens and branches. Decide what kinds of mechanical aids you need and have them ready.

To begin, anchor the holder in the container if necessary; if you use foam, soak it until it is moist and pliable. Then add water, treated with a preservative, using only enough water to cover the bottoms of the stems while you make the arrangement. Do not be afraid to skimp: the health of cut flowers is unaffected by water level so long as stem ends are immersed. A peony can drink from a thimbleful of water.

PLACING THE FLOWERS

Put your central flowers, greens or branches, often the longest ones, in position first, for they establish the basic height of your design *(pages 72-79)*. If the design calls for a curved stem or green that you do not have, you can wire or otherwise manipulate the material until you achieve the desired shape *(page 62)*.

After you have placed the central stems and branches, add those that will define the width of the arrangement. If you are making a centerpiece or other grouping that will be seen from all angles, add material to the front and back as well as at the sides. Finally, add the flowers that form the focus. When inserting flower stems into foam, push them into it only far enough to hold them in position, not through to the other side.

Keep checking your arrangement with a critical eye as you assemble it. Take your time, and do not hesitate to deviate from your original plan if you find that it can be improved upon. Finally, add the minor flowers, light greens and other filler material, making sure that they conceal the mechanical devices. If they do not, use moss or larger leaves to camouflage the holder. Exercise restraint at this point; you can easily spoil a good flower arrangement by adding too much extra material just because it happens to be available.

If you are making an old-fashioned massive bouquet with a great many flowers and greens, you may not need any holder to anchor it. Instead of starting with the tallest branches, begin by positioning the shorter material that will splay out around the bottom of the arrangement: the crisscrossed stems will serve as a holder for the longer stems and branches you add to the center of the arrangement. But be aware that such arrangements do not have as much stability as those that are made with metal or foam holders to keep the materials in place, so move them carefully.

FLOWER-DRYING METHODS

1. *To air-dry herbs such as rosemary, seed pods such as columbine, or wiry-stemmed flowers such as statice and babies'-breath, suspend loose bunches in a warm, dry, dark place.*

2. *Use silica gel, available at most florists, to dry dahlias, zinnias and other large, soft-petaled flowers. Fit cardboard supports crosswise in a lidded box and add an inch of gel. Remove foliage and rest the flowers on the supports, tucking in a stemless test flower. Cover the flowers with gel. Seal the lid on with tape. After two days check the test flower; when it is dry remove the other flowers.*

3. *Delicate flower stems that are brittle when dried should be cut off before flower heads are put in gel. Push florist's wire through the remaining bit of stem into the plump calyx beneath the petals, leaving an inch or so protruding (top left), or insert the wire crosswise (top right). Place face up on a bed of gel (bottom). Cover with more gel and replace the lid.*

4. *To provide cut-off and dried flower heads with false stems, twist ends of the short supporting wire together (right). Then twist on a double length of wire (center). Wrap the wires with florist's tape, winding from the top down (right).*

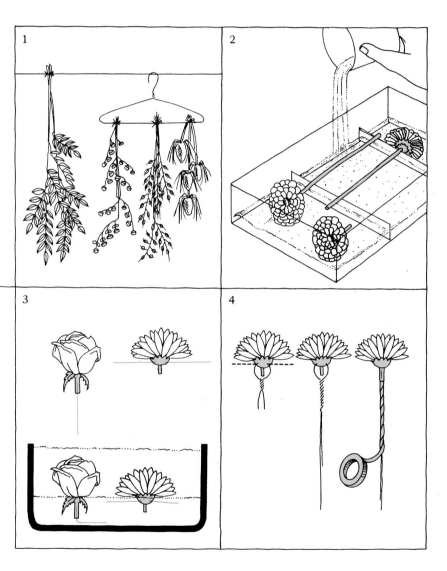

Once you have completed an arrangement, fill the container with water; you may be surprised by how much the flowers use. Give the arrangement a gentle misting and keep it out of direct sunlight and drafts and away from hot air. Check its water level twice daily and add more if it is necessary. The flowers will last longer and stay even fresher if you change the water daily; the quickest and easiest way to do this without disturbing the arrangement is to use a bulb-type kitchen baster. Move the arrangement to a cool place each night. With care, an arrangement will almost certainly last a week, and may last two.

The relatively short life of arrangements of freshly cut flowers is one of their most agreeable characteristics: you do not have to wait long before trying something new, perhaps in another place in the room. But if you want something that will be more permanent, dried arrangements that are composed of flowers, foliage and grasses have their own special pleasures.

DRIED ARRANGEMENTS

You can dry flowers by hanging them—allowing warm air to evaporate the moisture they contain—or by burying them in a drying agent such as sand, cornmeal, borax or silica gel. Hanging is an effective method for grasses, seed pods and flowers that have clumps of tiny blossoms, such as yarrow and goldenrod. To air-dry any of these materials, tie their stems in small bunches with elastic bands, then suspend them from a string or clothes hanger *(opposite page)* in a dry, dark area that is well ventilated. Most of these materials will dry within a week.

Sand is one of the oldest drying agents for flowers. In 1602, Sir Hugh Plat wrote these instructions for drying roses with sand in his *Delights for Ladies:* "Take the right Callis sand, wash it in some change of waters, and drie it thorowly well, either in an oven or in the sunne; and having shallow boxes of four, five or six inches deep, make first an even lay of sand, upon which lay your Roses-leaves, one by one till you have covered all the sand. Set this box in some warm place in a hot, sunnie day, and commonly in two hot, sunnie days they will be thorow drie."

MATERIALS FOR DRYING

Sand is still widely used, but it has been supplanted in popularity as a drying agent by silica gel, a modern material that removes moisture more quickly. (A quicker drying time generally means a truer blossom color.) Silica gel is also lighter in weight than sand, which may flatten delicate petals. Borax and cornmeal, two other common drying agents, sometimes cake and stick to the flowers, and borax can also burn petals.

Silica gel, which is sold by most florists, looks and feels much like sugar; it is used in industry to protect delicate instruments and dehydrated food from dampness. It can absorb up to 40 per cent of its weight in water. The silica gel sold for drying flowers contains gel crystals mixed with larger crystals of a nickel compound that is dark blue when it is dry. As the gel absorbs moisture from the plant materials, the crystals turn from light blue to pink, an indication that the gel has become saturated. To dry damp silica gel, place it in a flat pan in a 250° oven for about 30 minutes. The gel is ready for reuse when the crystals have turned dark blue again. Dry silica gel must be stored in an airtight container so it will not be able to absorb any moisture from the air.

Flowers to be dried should be cut at the driest time of a sunny day—midafternoon—but they should be conditioned overnight like fresh flowers so they will go into the drying process not moisture-laden but crisp and healthy. To dry flowers, you will need a metal or plastic box that has a tight cover. It should be deep enough to hold the flowers without crushing them, and you will need enough silica gel to fill it. Strip the foliage from the stem; if the stem is delicate and likely to be brittle when dry, sever it a half inch below the flower; replace it with an artificial stem *(page 66)*. Dry the blossoms, dabbing them very gently with the corner of a paper towel to remove any stray droplets.

DRY BUT NOT BRITTLE
Put a 1-inch layer of gel in the box and gently set the flowers down. Place blossoms with a single layer of petals, such as daisies, face down, rounded or trumpet-shaped flowers face up, flower spikes or clusters on their sides. Make sure no blossoms touch each other. Place a test flower in one corner of the box where you can easily find it for periodic checking; blooms that are left too long in the gel become too brittle to use. Finally, take a handful of gel and sift it slowly through your fingers until the flowers are gently covered, then put the lid on the box and seal it with masking or freezer tape. Silica gel dries most flowers in 24 to 48 hours, but the time needed varies with the kind of flower; optimum times are given in the encyclopedia entries that begin on page 111.

When the test flower has dried to a point where it is stiff but still springy, remove the rest of the flowers, letting the gel run slowly out of the box and gently brushing away any residue that clings to individual blossoms. If any petals fall off, you can reattach them with white household glue applied with a toothpick. Dried flowers are weaker than their fresh counterparts, of course, and to extend their life you can reinforce all the petal joinings by brushing on a thin mixture of white glue and water. After the glue has dried, make artificial stems if they are needed, using wire covered with florist's tape. The flowers are then ready for arranging.

Wreathed in nature's bounty

A ring-shaped base of sphagnum moss or straw, available at flower shops, is the starting point for a richly decorated holiday wreath. Once the base has been covered with evergreen sprigs *(right)*, add some natural materials—apples, nuts, cones—to produce a design that can be as simple or as elegant as you like *(below)*.

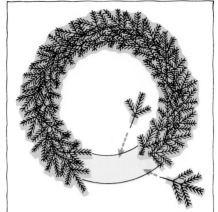

Insert a 6-inch sprig into the base *(left)* so it overlaps the outer edge. Next insert a shorter sprig near the first, but overlapping the inner edge. Work around the base in one direction, alternately adding sprigs pointing in and out. To make the job easier, strip off the needles near the end of each sprig. Soften a sphagnum-moss base with hot water before starting.

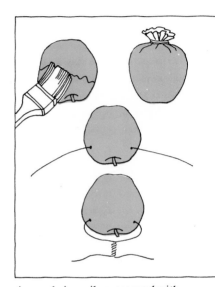

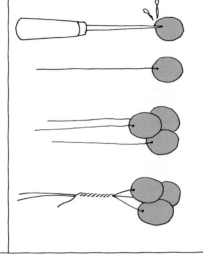

An apple is easily preserved with shellac *(top left)* or with stretchable plastic wrap tied at the stem end *(top right)*. For a hanger, run a wire through the apple near the stem end *(center)* and twist the ends.

To add a hanger to a nut, first burn a hole in one end with a heated ice pick *(top)* or awl. Dip a wire in glue; push it into the hole *(center)*. When the glue is hard, group a few nuts and twist the wires together *(bottom)*.

To make pine-cone rosettes, cut a cone into sections with pruning shears or a small saw *(top)*. Slip wire under the lower scales and twist the ends together *(left)*. To make a bouquet, twist several wires together *(right)*.

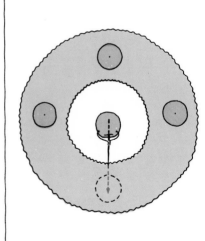

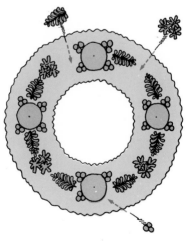

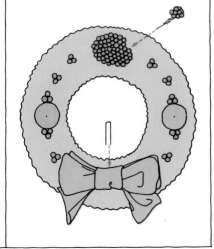

Near the stem end of a prepared apple, insert the square end of a 3- to 4-inch florist's pick. Wind the wires around the pick. Then push the pick into the wreath just as you would stick a pin into a pincushion.

Fill out your design with nuts, cones and cone rosettes, winding their wires around florist's picks or the smaller, hairpin-like florist's pins. A symmetrical design is shown, but a freer one can be as attractive.

To simulate a bunch of grapes, attach wired nut clusters to florist's picks and pin them to the wreath so they touch each other *(top)*. Use water-repellent ribbon to make a bow and fasten it with a florist's pin *(bottom)*.

Some arrangers actually prefer working with dried flowers because they are so easily held in place in a container. All you need is a block of dry brown foamed plastic (not green floral foam, which crumbles when dry). Simply push the stems into this foam and hide the base with dried moss or leaves. You will find that mixing colors is easier with dried flowers because their hues are muted and blend readily. Blue, orange and pink blossoms tend to retain most of their color after drying, while reds and purples may darken, yellows and greens fade, and whites turn cream or beige.

Dried flowers will last for many years, but even if you just want to keep a dried arrangement for a few months, you should protect it from high humidity with a squirt of hair spray or plastic fixative to keep it looking fresh.

Foliage and flowers can also be preserved by pressing, which works best on flat flowers such as daisies and pansies, and on most leaves. Place a layer of newspaper on a board and cover the newspaper with a thin layer of silica gel. Spread two thicknesses of white facial tissue over the gel and place the flowers or leaves on the tissue. Then reverse the sandwich, adding layers of tissue, gel and newspaper. Seal the board and its sandwich in a large plastic bag and cover the top of the sandwich with books or bricks. In a week or so, the materials will have dried.

PRESERVING WITH GLYCERIN

Many arrangers preserve branches of foliage by saturating them with glycerin. This works well with woody-stemmed boughs of holly, laurel, magnolia, rhododendron, leucothoë and wild huckleberry, and for branches of most fruit trees and conifers. You can gather mature foliage for treatment any time from late spring to late fall, but late summer is generally the best time, when leaves are neither too young nor too old to respond. Make sure the foliage is clean, then split the branch ends up to 2 inches to increase the area available for absorption of the glycerin. Stand the branches in a container filled with a solution of 1 part glycerin to 2 parts water. The branches will absorb sufficient glycerin (available at most drug stores) in one to three weeks to preserve the foliage indefinitely. Add more solution as necessary. When you see tiny drops of glycerin at the ends of the leaves, saturation is complete. Remove the branches from the solution and hang them upside down to dry for at least two weeks before using them in an arrangement.

Foliage preserved in this manner will have a lustrous shine, but it may change color—bayberry, for example, turns red when treated in the spring and brown in the fall. Leaves of leucothoë branches cut in the fall turn deep bronze. After treatment with glycerin, foliage is colorfast and will last for years.

Forcing—stimulating spring-flowering trees and shrubs to blossom in midwinter or early spring, long before their normal blooming time—is another technique that can be put to good use by the flower arranger. Generally, the closer to the normal outdoor blooming season a branch is forced, the faster its buds will open. The buds of a plant that is completely dormant rarely will respond to forcing, but if some swelling of buds is evident, it is worthwhile cutting a branch and trying to force it, even in the dead of winter.

To increase your chances of success, cut branches with an abundance of buds on a day when the temperature is above freezing. Slit the cut ends of the branches with a knife to increase the absorption of water, and lay the branches in a tub of tepid water overnight. Then keep the branches moist by wrapping them in wet newspaper and placing them upright in a vase of tepid water. Leave them wrapped in a cool place until the buds begin to show some color. Then remove the newspaper and place the vase in a cool, bright place, but not in direct sunlight. Mist the branches frequently with room-temperature water and you soon will be rewarded with flowers. The blossoms will be no less colorful than their later outdoor counterparts, and their early appearance as a foretaste of spring makes them doubly welcome.

FORCING BLOOMS IN WINTER

SUPPORTING STEMS AND BRANCHES

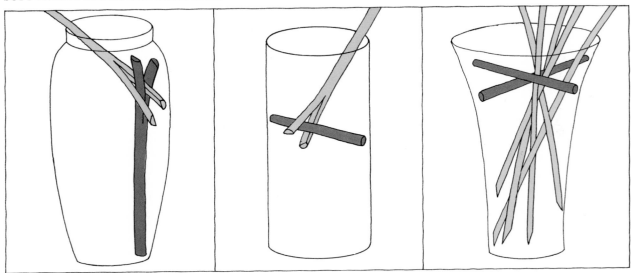

If you are using a narrow-mouthed vase, make a prop for an angled branch by splitting one end of a woody stem shorter than the vase. Also split the branch being positioned, then wedge the pair of stems against the side, bottom and rim of the vase.

For a straight-sided vase, cut a piece of woody stem slightly longer than the vase diameter. Split the stem you are positioning and wedge the prop into it. Work the prop into the vase until it is wedged between the sides. Rest the projecting stem on the rim of the vase.

To simplify arranging flowers in a vase that has a flaring mouth, cut two pieces of woody stems long enough to be wedged in snugly, in the form of a cross, just below the water line. Arrange flowers in any or all of the quadrants that are thus formed.

Eleven ways to shape bouquets

Although flower arranging is a personal pursuit, there are guidelines developed by professionals for shaping basic Western mass arrangements and the more complex Oriental line compositions.

These guidelines are illustrated on the following pages in diagrams that show you how to construct basic shapes step by step—from the placement of the first flower to the placement of the last. Once you have mastered these basic shapes, you will be able to design your own variations.

To form any of the shapes illustrated, position the flowers in the sequence in which they are numbered in the diagrams. The colors red, blue and black are used to distinguish the major stages in constructing the design. In an actual arrangement, of course, the flowers can be any color.

The accompanying photographs interpret rather than reproduce the diagrams precisely, since individual flowers will tilt and balance in different ways. Similarly, the diagrams show solid silhouettes, but a skilled arranger will vary any basic outline with airy or linear materials that will add different textures, movement and drama. Even the shapes are not immutable; the crescent and S-curve arrangements on pages 76-77 work equally well if curved in the opposite direction, and a crescent shape can be transformed into an L shape by using straight rather than curved stems.

Most of these arrangements are designed for viewing from one side, but you can make them attractive from the back by duplicating the design on the other side of the container, using outline flowers that face in both directions. As the photographs show, many garden flowers can be used in all styles of arrangements. Most of the shapes are suitable for dried flowers as well; you just use more pieces to compensate for their shrunken size and subdued color.

Choosing a shape is only the first step, however. A successful design—whether Western or Oriental—also needs color, rhythm, balance and scale. How an Ikebana designer puts his personal stamp on formalized shapes is illustrated on pages 80-83.

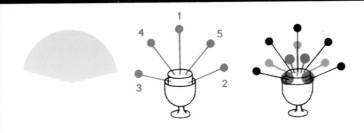

FAN ARRANGEMENT

THE DIAGRAMS. *The basic outline for a fan arrangement consists of five spokelike stems of equal length. Place the first stem (1) upright in the center, with supporting spokes (2 and 3) angling upward on each side. Add another pair (4 and 5), then fill in with shorter flowers, shown (right) in blue and red.*

THE PHOTOGRAPH. *Juniper and freesia form the main spokes of the fan in this example. Anemone and dahlia complete the outline and lead the eye to a brilliant dahlia left of center.*

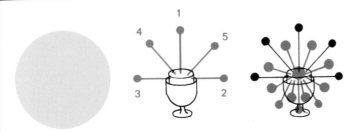

CIRCULAR ARRANGEMENT

THE DIAGRAMS. *The basic outline for a circular arrangement is the same as for a fan, except that here spokes 2 and 3 project horizontally from the raised flower holder. Fill in the outline with round flowers, some projecting downward to mask the rim of the container. Complete the arrangement on all sides.*

THE PHOTOGRAPH. *French marigolds and Queen Anne's lace round the outline. A bold pink cosmos draws attention at lower left, balanced by pink ranunculuses (upper right).*

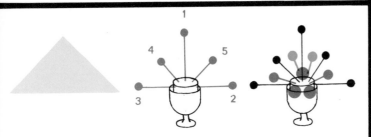

TRIANGULAR ARRANGEMENT

THE DIAGRAMS. *Follow the steps for the circular outline except that stems 4 and 5 must be shorter than stem 1. Add pieces 2 and 3, finishing the outline with spike or round shapes (4 and 5). Use round flowers in the center (blue, then red).*

THE PHOTOGRAPH. *In a demure arrangement of alba lilies and narcissuses, splashes of red nerine and freesia move the eye from outline to core. Asparagus fern and gray-green euphorbia overhang the rim and soften the formal shape.*

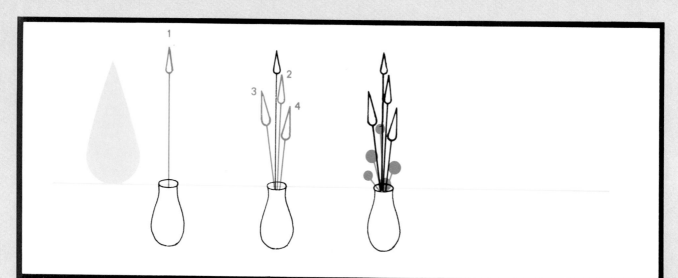

VERTICAL ARRANGEMENT

THE DIAGRAMS. *Launch a vertical arrangement with a single spike-shaped flower, bud or leaf (1), flanking it with three progressively shorter spikes (2 through 4) to form a tapering outline. Then plump the center section with as many round flowers as you want. Balance the soaring vertical line with a large round shape at the base of the arrangement. If you use a tall vase with a narrow mouth, you may not need a flower holder.*

THE PHOTOGRAPH. *A pale pink rosebud with an upturned leaf was the starting point for the arrangement at right. It is supported by half-opened yellow roses. Acacia, brodiaea and Peruvian lilies fill the center of the shape. At the base, two fat rosettes of pink nerine repeat, in a deeper hue, the color of the top rose.*

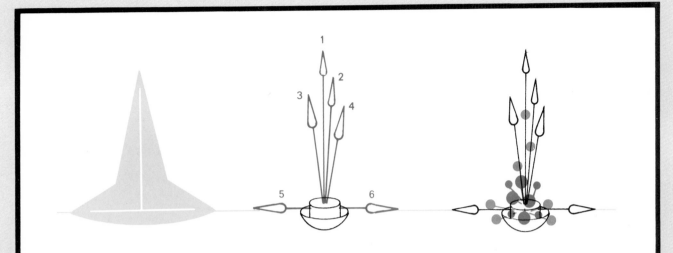

INVERTED T ARRANGEMENT

THE DIAGRAMS. *Start an inverted T arrangement with the flower holder raised above the container rim. Position a spike-shaped flower or piece of foliage (1) in the center of the flower holder, cutting the stem to a length that is more than twice the diameter of a low container or more than one and one half times the height of a tall container. Then add slightly shorter elements (2 through 4). Use either round or spike shapes cut shorter than 4 to outline the horizontal arms (5 and 6). Add four round flowers shorter than these arms to project horizontally on either side, then add other round flowers of increasing lengths (blue) to fill in the vertical outline. For balance, add more round flowers (red) at the base.*

THE PHOTOGRAPH. *A star-of-Bethlehem spire marks the top of the T, followed by speckled Peruvian lilies and a half-open orange calendula. Full-blown calendulas balance the arms of the T, formed by spears of star-of-Bethlehem and spiky euphorbia leaves. Asparagus fern, Peruvian lilies and white brodiaea stabilize the center while larger blossoms of anemone, Tabasco lily and nerine climb toward the top of the arrangement.*

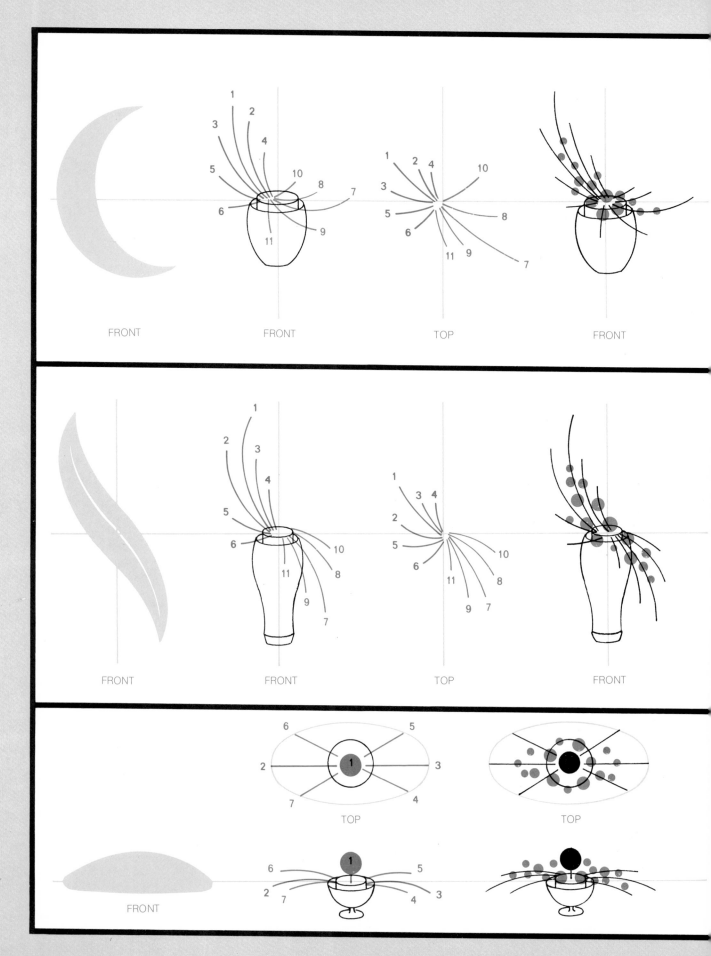

FRONT FRONT TOP FRONT

FRONT FRONT TOP FRONT

TOP TOP

FRONT

CRESCENT ARRANGEMENT

THE DIAGRAMS. *Start a crescent arrangement with a stem (1) that has a strong curve, fixing it securely in the flower holder slightly to the left of center. Using spike-shaped foliage or flowers to emphasize the outline, cut stems 2 through 6 progressively shorter and shape them (page 62) to follow the curve of the first, inserting them alternately on either side. The top view shows front-to-back placement. In the lower half of the crescent, stem 7 continues the line of stem 1, with shorter pieces (8 through 11) branching off on either side. Use round flowers (blue) to add fullness to the outline; place larger flowers (red) near the top of the container for stability.*

THE PHOTOGRAPH. *Spikes of star-of-Bethlehem trace the sweep of the crescent from tip to tip. Delicate blooms and foliage of acacia and Queen Anne's lace support the curve, with two half-opened amaryllises to balance and embellish the design.*

S-CURVE ARRANGEMENT

THE DIAGRAMS. *Position the primary curved stem (1) in the center of a raised flower holder, placing progressively shorter stems 2 through 6 on each side to form the top half of the S. In the bottom half, stem 7 reverses the curve begun above by stem 1. Stems 8 through 11 fill out the bottom curve on each side. The tips of the S curve (1 and 7) should be approximately the same distance from an imaginary vertical line bisecting the arrangement. Use small flowers (blue) to make transitions within the principal lines and fill the center of the design with larger round flowers (red).*

THE PHOTOGRAPH. *Two pliant branches of small-flowered euphorbia form the dominant line of the S, supported by rosettes of red nerine and white brodiaea at the top and sprigs of freesia and juniper at the bottom. A large red dahlia provides a pivot for the arrangement at the center, balanced by smaller dahlias on either side.*

HORIZONTAL ARRANGEMENT

THE DIAGRAMS. *In the middle of a low bowl, start a horizontal arrangement by positioning a short round flower (1), then add longer horizontal spikes (2 and 3) on each side. Complete the outline with shorter pairs of spike-shaped flowers or foliage (4 through 7) to form an oval shape (top view). Group small round flowers (blue) toward the outer edge, facing them in all directions so the design is pleasing from any angle. Fill the central area with larger blossoms (red).*

THE PHOTOGRAPH. *Spikes of snapdragon and star-of-Bethlehem extend gracefully from this low arrangement, framing a cluster of calendula, ranunculus and Queen Anne's lace.*

Ikebana: a natural unity of three

From the beginning of their ancient nature worship, Shinto, the Japanese have tended to distill universal elements into basic trinities. In the 17th Century, in flower arranging, the Japanese began to use three elements to signify the relationship between man and nature: the longest branch symbolizes heaven and the shortest the earth, with man represented by the branch in the middle.

The names assigned to these elements survive today for practical rather than metaphysical reasons. Ikebana diagrams such as those below use a circle to denote the heaven line, a square for the man line

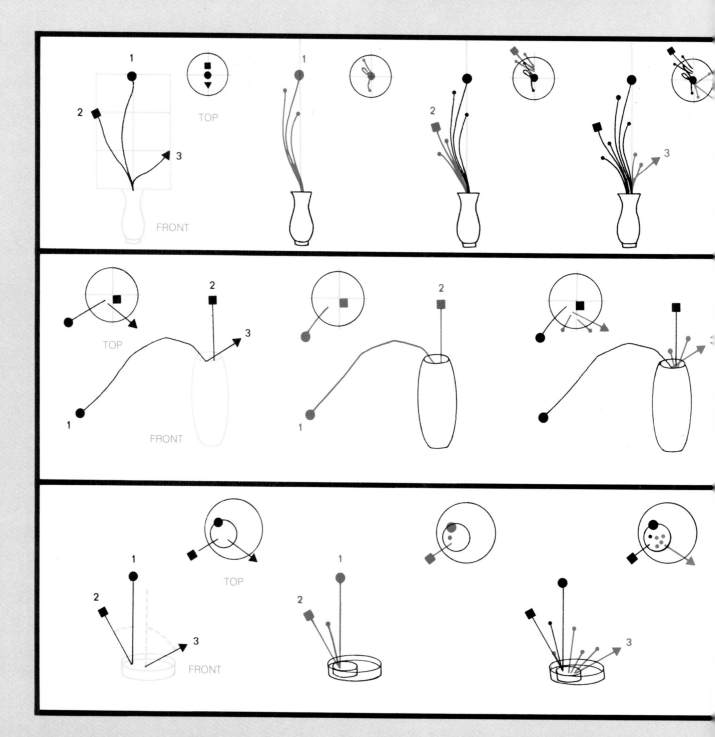

and a triangle for earth. The length of the stems reflects a plant's stage of development. The longest stem of an iris, for example, having had the most time to grow, has the most fully developed flowers.

The Japanese desire to reflect nature can also be seen in the orientation of flowers. In Ikebana, leaves and blossoms are placed so the flower is upright or slightly inclined as if growing toward the sun.

The styles illustrated are the shoka arrangement of the 17th Century *(top)*, an 18th Century nageire *(center)* and a Western-influenced low moribana of the late 19th Century *(bottom)*.

SHOKA STYLE

THE DIAGRAMS. *In a shoka arrangement, three curved branches rise in a front-to-back row (front views). The heaven line is half again as tall as the vase; the man line is two thirds as tall and the earth line one third as tall as the heaven line. In a tall vase, place the heaven line (1) so its tip aligns with the vase's center, adding similarly curving supplementary material. Then place the man and earth lines (2 and 3) so they extend equally in opposite directions (top views). Add supplementary material if desired.*

THE PHOTOGRAPH. *Golden marguerites aspire toward purple irises, seeming to mirror their vibrant accent color.*

NAGEIRE STYLE

THE DIAGRAMS. *Prune a distinctively curved branch to create a horizontal heaven line (1), fixing it with a wooden support (page 71). Position the man line (2) upright and slightly toward the opposite side (top view, center). The short earth line (3) needs a large, dramatic blossom to offset the pull of the heaven line, and is often assisted by one or two similar flowers (front view, right).*

THE PHOTOGRAPH. *A red chokeberry branch, bent to accentuate its natural curve, slants outward to form the heaven line and upward to form the man line. Red anemones, the higher one representing earth, counterbalance the branch.*

MORIBANA STYLE

THE DIAGRAMS. *Using a pinholder, fix the heaven line (1) near the back or one side of a low container. Then position the man line (2) at a 45° angle to one side. Fill the spaces between these two and in the center of the container with some supplementary flowers before anchoring the earth line (3) at a 60° angle in the front.*

THE PHOTOGRAPH. *Orange lilies, their leaves overhanging the container edge, represent the three basic Ikebana elements, but they frame a Western-style mass of daisies.*

Ikebana expert Mutsuo Tomita prunes an elegantly crooked branch of star magnolia for the man line of a nageire arrangement.

An artist's telling touch

Mutsuo Tomita, of New York's Ohara School of Ikebana, shows five variations within the prescribed forms. His slanting *nageire* *(left)*, incorporates a traditional Western rose. The other arrangements are Tomita's low-bowl *moribana* designs: two in the heavenly form *(below)*, two in the landscape form *(overleaf)*.

Viburnum berries brighten an airy, naturalistic arrangement in an earthen bowl; a slender reed stretches heavenward, its apparent weightlessness offsetting its height.

Looping gladiolus leaves, dampened so they could be bent, accentuate the undulating flower stalk. Fully opened flowers at the base reveal a Western influence in this design.

Juniper branches, club moss and sprigs
of goldenrod simulate a grove of
trees on a distant, flower-banked shore.
The rectangular suiban bowl, used
commonly in landscape arrangements,
contains very little water, so it
accurately reflects the Japanese dry
season in fall.

Cockscomb punctuates with blazing
color the three principal lines in this
arrangement. Foxtail and pokeweed
add movement to the scene, based
on a landscape viewed close-up at
water's edge. The rim of the ceramic
bowl is based on the design of an
ancient Japanese mirror.

Gardens that go anywhere

4

Outdoor container gardening is for people who change their minds. If your flower, shrub or tree is in a pot, tub, box, urn or hanging basket separated from the earth, you can move it around to experiment endlessly with decorative effects. If one scheme does not work, you can try another. You can rearrange your portable garden to suit the seasons or special occasions, or merely to satisfy a whim. For an apartment dweller with a small balcony or rooftop, a condominium owner with only a terrace, or a suburban townhouse resident with a backyard barely large enough to turn around in, container gardening may be the only kind of outdoor gardening possible.

Even if you have a conventional garden, the use of containers opens new horizons. Container-grown flowering plants can provide a movable feast of color; one Midwesterner, for example, keeps several potted pink Fiat Enchantress geraniums on hand to perk up her flower beds when perennials are not in bloom. Container plants are often healthier than their earth-bound counterparts because each can have a tailor-made soil mixture, mulch and watering regimen. And if you move, you can take them with you.

Terraces, porches and balconies are outdoor rooms, so in choosing and placing plants apply the same considerations as for other rooms in your home: color, shape, scale, texture and the way plants blend with their surroundings and their containers. There are some differences, however. Outdoor plants will usually be larger than indoor plants, and their containers must be tougher and heavier, made of concrete, wood, artificial stone or earthenware. On a terrace you may want an 8-foot tree growing in a box 3 feet square. There are significant differences in plant culture to be taken into account, too. Indoors, subtle adjustments in light and humidity may make the difference between success and failure; outdoors such adjustments are of a different magnitude, involving wind, sun, water and extremes of heat and cold.

Edging a driveway where the soil is too compacted for conventional planting, rows of potted yellow marigolds and lavender ageratums add depth and visual impact to a stand of earth-bound orange marigolds.

As you make your plans, note how much light reaches your terrace or balcony in each season, the high and low temperatures in summer and winter, and what shelter is provided by surrounding structures—overhead balconies, neighboring buildings, fences and walls, as well as trees and shrubs. Consider how you will use your outdoor room: will it be a place for dining, a center for hobbies and games or purely decorative? Visit garden centers and nurseries to find out what kinds of plants will fit your space and your budget. Make sketches, thinking not only of how the area will work while you are in it but how it will look from inside your home.

PLANTS FOR PLANTERS   You will find it easier to choose plants for your outdoor room if you consider them in three categories: the trees or shrubs that will dominate the design, the vines and ground covers that will serve as screens and background, and the smaller flowering plants that will add color. In most cases, your basic materials will be woody trees, shrubs and vines that can live outdoors all year long. A key question is whether to use evergreen or deciduous varieties. Evergreens retain their foliage through the winter, and none can deny the beauty of a snow-covered spruce in January. But they cannot survive without some care. Container-grown evergreens need watering through the winter and may need covering to protect them from drying wind or bitter cold. Deciduous trees in containers, including dwarf varieties of flowering fruit trees, are only slightly less appealing: the silhouette of bare branches against the sky has its own special charm. Deciduous trees need the same attention as evergreens; your nurseryman can tell you which trees and shrubs have the best chance of surviving your local winter in an outdoor container.

One thrifty apartment dweller in Washington, D.C., gets double enjoyment from the Scotch pine that he keeps in a balcony tub most of the year. "I bring it in for a short time every December," he says. "With a few decorations I have one of the nicest Christmas trees around. I have to water it more than usual indoors and I prune the roots back every couple of years to keep it small, but it's worth it. I never have to rush around looking for a tree. Have you ever tried to get into a cab with an 8-foot tree?"

Vines like the ivies and creeping euonymus are useful for blanketing walls, fences or balcony railings. Flowering varieties like clematis and honeysuckle can be as much a center of attention as any tree or shrub. Ground covers such as creeping myrtle, pachysandra and ajuga are handy for concealing the soil in large containers holding single specimen plants. More important are the smaller trees, shrubs and flowering plants that fill out container gardens: trees such as Japanese maples or junipers, shrubs such as rhododendron, forsythia, privet and camellia, and countless flowering perennials and annuals.

When you choose flowering plants, you will do best with annuals. Perennials are lovely in bloom, but for a good part of the summer most of them show only foliage. Annuals give a blaze of color month after month if you pick off faded blossoms before seed pods form, and they can be tossed on the compost pile or into the trash when the first frost arrives. With annuals, you can have a completely different display each year if you like.

Once you have decided what plants and containers will best decorate your outdoor room, you can begin to fit them into their new environment. Resist the temptation to pack them in. An abundance of plants may make your friends believe you have the greatest green thumb since Luther Burbank, but crowded plants that compete with each other are hard to care for and they are more subject to insect attack than those carefully spaced. Use just enough shapes and sizes to give variety without risking clutter, using the categories in the encyclopedia *(page 111)* as a guide. If you like, you can combine round and square containers, tall and short shrubs, bushy growth with lacy or spiky. But always maintain a focal point to unify your design—a single tree, shrub or group of plants worthy of concentrated attention. You can also use plants to solve architectural problems. For instance, a row of plants of varying heights will break up the monotony of a blank wall or screen out an unpleasant view, as will a trellis covered with vines, or baskets of trailing plants hung from a roof overhang.

No matter how you use plants to decorate outdoor rooms, be sure to provide protection from the extremes of sun and wind. If neighboring buildings and trees give inadequate shelter, you can provide shade when necessary with awnings or overhead lath structures, or with vines growing over an arbor. Trellises and board or stockade fences make good windbreaks, as do tall shrubs such as viburnum, lined up in matching containers.

At the outset, do not feel that you have to furnish an entire terrace or balcony all at once. As with any garden, begin with a few plants to get a feel for the materials you will be working with as your decorating becomes more elaborate. One place to start is your entranceway. Container plants flanking a doorway are always handsome, and you can change them to reflect the seasons. One Boston husband and wife rotate plants in and out of two graceful urns by their front door, presenting geraniums in summer, chrysanthemums or English ivy in the fall, evergreens at Christmas. If you have a front porch, it may be more inviting with hanging baskets of vines or

TRAINING A LIVING HOOP

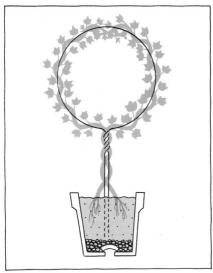

A hoop to support twining vines or those that cling with tendrils can be made by shaping a 4-foot length of 12-gauge wire around a pot or jug 12 to 14 inches in diameter, then twisting the ends together. Prepare an 8-inch pot for planting and push the twisted wire through the soil to the bottom of the pot. Set a rooted plant on either side of the support. When the vines reach the hoop, start them up opposite sides. When they meet at the top, pinch off the leaves along the vertical wires.

AN INVITING ENTRANCE

flowering annuals on either side of the door. Pathways and driveways can be lined with container plants.

For many city apartment dwellers, the only suitable outdoor space for container plants is a balcony. These attractive adjuncts challenge the gardener because they are usually narrow, and decorating them requires plants that take up little space—varieties that will climb up or hang down or skirt the outer edges. Window boxes can be hung from the inside of a balcony railing, holding several plants in a limited space without making them seem crowded. Even the smallest balcony has room for a container holding a shrub, a small tree or, for color, some flowers. Above all, do not overlook air space; by hanging plants from the balcony above or on brackets near the entrance, you will create a three-dimensional effect that gives a feeling of greater depth to the area, an important consideration for a small apartment.

BLOOMS IN MIDAIR

The great 18th Century English and French garden designers freely used hanging baskets of flowers to enhance their lavish landscapes, and a century later an 1872 Victorian gardening manual marveled at "how infinite, and yet indescribably beautiful, are some of the combinations of plants in baskets that we actually see." Hanging plants dropped in popularity as gardeners turned to other

MAKING A HANGING FERN BALL

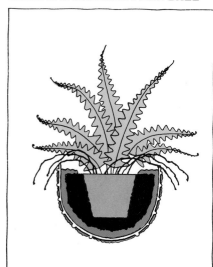  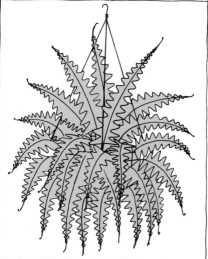

For a fern that sends out runners (like the Boston) or rhizomes (davallia), line a wire basket with a 2-inch layer of uncut sphagnum moss and fill it ⅓ full of potting soil. Set in the fern and fill around the edges with more soil.

To ensure a well-shaped ball, distribute the runners or rhizomes evenly around the outside of the basket. Attach each to a bit of moss at several points, using U-shaped wires. Cover the soil with more moss.

Attach a hanger to the basket and suspend it in a shady location. Keep the soil moist to the touch and rotate the ball from time to time to keep growth symmetrical. In a month or two, runners or rhizomes will root.

innovations, but they made a strong comeback with the introduction of containers with attached saucers that made care easier.

Hanging plants can be used indoors as well as out, of course. If dripping water is of no concern, such plants do well in wire baskets lined with sphagnum moss and filled with potting soil *(pages 90-93)*. But for most indoor locations you will need more conventional pots and saucers to catch the water that runs through.

Technically, any plant can be suspended, though it is usually impractical to hang very large ones, and most that grow upright must be planted at an awkward 45° angle to thrive in hanging containers. Plants that tend to trail over the sides of pots, such as tuberous begonias, fuchsias, petunias and ivies, are good candidates for outdoor hanging baskets, as are bushy impatiens and browallias. Trailing varieties of annuals and perennials presented this way afford the outdoor gardener a breathtaking display of color. One Boston family keeps more than 250 moss-lined baskets blooming in a 12-by-20-foot yard throughout the summer, suspending such disparate plants as bougainvilleas, ivy geraniums, columneas and orchids at various heights from a solitary maple tree and several patio brackets.

In the spring, many nurseries sell hanging baskets containing plants that are already blossoming, but you may want to plant your

CANDIDATES FOR SUSPENSION

MAKING A HANGING FLOWER BALL

To create a flower ball, line a wire basket with 2 inches of uncut sphagnum moss, then add 2 inches of potting soil and firm it. Make holes through the moss and insert small wax begonias so root balls rest on soil.

Position plants 5 to 6 inches apart to make a ring around the basket. Cover roots with 2 inches of soil, then plant a ring bearing contrasting flowers. On top, plant upright flowers that are a third color.

Suspend the basket and water it well. Hang the flower ball outdoors in a spot sheltered from the wind. Rotate the basket every few days so all plants will get equal amounts of light. Keep the soil moist.

own. For example, you may have a single 4-inch pot of trailing lantana or fuchsia that you want to transfer to an outdoor basket. You will need a 10- or 12-inch round-bottomed wire basket, enough uncut sphagnum moss to make a 2-inch lining and a mix of 2 parts packaged potting soil to 1 part peat moss. If you start with garden loam, make the mix of 1 part peat moss and 1 part sand, vermiculite or perlite to each part of soil.

GARDENING IN A BASKET

Soak the sphagnum moss in warm water for half an hour, squeeze it until it is just moist, and apply it in handfuls to the inside of the basket, wedging it between the frame wires and filling in empty spaces until you have completely lined the basket to a 2-inch depth. Build the lining up to a level about an inch above the wire rim, then inspect it for gaps by holding the basket up to the light. It should look like one of those Russian fur hats turned upside down. Add potting soil to the lined basket until the top of your plant's root ball will be about ½ inch below the wire rim. Position the plant and fill in the space around it with soil, firming the soil with your fingers and making the surface level, then fold down the sphagnum moss liner so that no soil will escape.

Set the basket in a tub of water that comes about halfway up its sides, but leave it there only until the surface soil is moist. Set it aside to drain in a shady, sheltered spot for three or four days before moving it to its permanent location. The plant will grow out rapidly and its blooms will soon hang down on all sides. Because its exposed soil dries rapidly, your outdoor basket will need frequent watering: once a day most of the year and more often than that when the weather is hot or windy.

(continued on page 94)

Hanging a window garden

Plants suspended artfully in space add drama and dimension to any setting—particularly windows, where their light needs are most easily satisfied. But there is more to hanging a plant than simply attaching its pot or basket to a ceiling hook. For one thing, hanging plants are bathed with rising warm air so they dry out faster than other plants do. One gardener solved this problem by concentrating on cacti and succulents (page 92), plants that flourish with minimum humidity in the strong, direct light of a south window. (For a comparison of sunlight intensity at different exposures, see page 16.)

The height at which a plant is placed is also important. The north-facing French windows on page 93 hold a miniature rain forest in which the plants are placed as they might be found in nature: shade-loving plants of the forest floor are clustered near the window sill, but orchids and bromeliads are hung higher where they get a bit more of the limited indirect light. The main reason hanging baskets have become so popular, however, is that they efficiently use otherwise wasted space, filling a window like the one opposite with a curtain of greenery and color from sill to ceiling.

Supported by nearly invisible nylon fishing line, a spiky yellow pachystachys is hung next to a trailing columnea (upper right); begonias (left) are hung so low they seem to be on the sill. All these plants thrive in a southern exposure.

91

*A stringy hatiora cactus (top left), a burro's tail (center),
three Christmas cacti in bloom on the sill and other desert
plants bask in strong southern light reflected from a mirrored
table and only slightly reduced by a glass-beaded curtain.*

An oncidium orchid (below the Boston fern) and a
strapping paphiopedilum orchid (above the ferns at right) are in
this north window because they will bloom in low light. The
floor plants are set in concealed humidity trays.

Hanging plants that can be purchased from nurseries for indoor display range from verdant tropicals like peperomias and spider plants to succulents such as burro's tails, vines such as creeping figs, wispy arching ferns, or spectacular African violets and ivy geraniums. These plants usually come in lightweight plastic containers complete with drainage saucers and wire hangers. Undeniably efficient, such containers have spurred interest in hanging plants, and if your plant is a luxuriant grower like a tradescantia, you can keep it in the utilitarian pot that it came in because the foliage will soon conceal the container.

If you should decide to move your plant on to something more decorative, remember that containers suspended in the air are particularly visible. Plastic and clay are the most popular materials for hanging containers, plastic because it is light and retains moisture well in an exposed outdoor location, clay because it is porous enough to let oxygen into the root zone and to let excess water evaporate indoors. If your scheme calls for a more decorative container, try glazed or painted pots, which hold moisture better than unglazed ones. Metal and glass usually are impractical: metal heats up in warm weather and glass is fragile. As a general rule you should use a saucer-equipped pot with a drainage hole. Good drainage is more important than good looks; if you use a container without a drainage hole, line the bottom with 2 or 3 inches of gravel, pebbles or clay-pot shards, add some charcoal, and be prepared to take extra care in watering to be sure the potting mixture does not become soggy.

Supporting a heavy hanging plant presents a challenge, but one that can be a pleasure to meet. Hangers made of clear nylon make a plant seem to float in midair. Wire or chain hangers are serviceable. And some macramé weavings are so handsome that hobbyists hang plants just to display the hangers (you do need to be careful not to wet such hangers, since they may rot). Whatever kind of hanger you use, be sure it is anchored securely to an integral part of the house indoors—a beam, joist, stud or window frame—or to a strong tree limb or overhang outdoors.

CHOOSING A CONTAINER

Combining beauty with practicality is also a major consideration when you select earth-bound outdoor containers for your larger plants. They should be durable, weatherproof and stable, with a low center of gravity so the wind will not tip them over. Any outdoor container should also be movable, either by lifting or by pushing it around on rollers or skids. Clay pots are most popular for small plants, though they sometimes crack if left outdoors in the winter where the soil alternately freezes and thaws. Among the unglazed pots, you can use standard ones, which are slightly taller than they

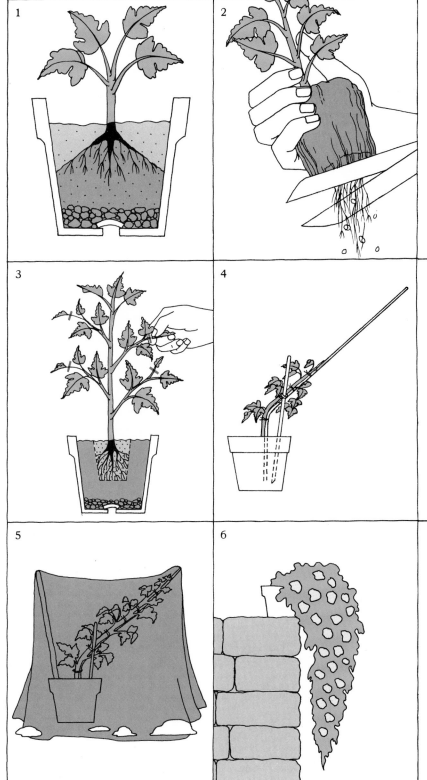

AN OUTDOOR CASCADING MUM

1. *To produce a cascading chrysanthemum, start in early spring with a rooted cutting of a tall, sprawling variety with pliable stems. Plant it in a 4-inch clay pot, using 2 parts potting soil, 1 part peat moss and 1 part sand. Drape bare roots over a cone of mix, then add more mix. Water well and set the plant in outdoor shade for three days, then in the sun.*

2. *When roots poke through the drainage hole, trim off long roots and move the plant to the next larger pot size. Keep the soil moist and feed weekly with half-strength house-plant fertilizer.*

3. *As side shoots develop, pinch off the tip growth on each just above the third leaf. Continue to pinch off new shoots to keep the narrow shape.*

4. *When the plant is 12 to 15 inches tall, stake the main stem with a 3-foot length of 12-gauge wire. Tie the two together with plant ties at 3-inch intervals. Carefully bend stem and wire to a 40° angle about 6 inches above the soil. Stop watering two days before bending; the stem may snap if it is full of water. Support the wire and stem with another stake. Point the plant's tip north so its surface will get enough light to form buds.*

5. *In areas where killing frost is due in October, use an opaque cloth supported by stakes from mid-August on to cover the plant each day at 4 p.m. and leave covered until morning. Weight the edges to exclude all light. These artificially lengthened nights will cause flower buds to form ahead of their normal schedule. Stop pinching when you begin this treatment.*

6. *When the buds begin to show color, set the pot on a wall and gently bend the wire and stem downward to form the cascade, with buds facing the sun. In mild areas with long autumns, do not cover, and stop pinching in mid-September.*

are wide, or the lower azalea pots, which are wider than they are tall. Unglazed pots can be pleasing to the eye outdoors, but be sure they have drainage holes; any that do not must be drilled. If the hole is in the bottom, the pot must be propped up to drain properly; drilled holes can be positioned on the side near the bottom.

For larger plants, shrubs and trees, containers made of wood are the choice of many garden designers and decorators. Redwood, cypress and cedar are popular for this purpose because they are light, strong and naturally rot-resistant. You can also use pine or other softwood if you coat it with a garden type of wood preservative such as copper naphthenate. Do not use creosote or pentachlorophenol, which are harmful to plants.

Other materials to consider are plastic, fiberglass, asbestos and concrete. Light, strong plastic is useful if weight is a concern, as on a rooftop. Fiberglass and asbestos containers are light and durable, but they are more expensive.

MAKING A CONCRETE PLANTER

Concrete, too heavy for most balconies or rooftops, is useful whenever weight is not a problem. It will last indefinitely. Garden centers sell good concrete tubs and boxes, often made with a lightweight aggregate like vermiculite to make them more portable.

If you like, you can easily make your own concrete planter. You will need two cardboard boxes to serve as forms, a larger one for the outside surfaces and a smaller one for the inside, some chicken wire with 2-inch mesh for reinforcing, dowels and ready-mix cement. First, cut some drainage holes in the bottom of the smaller box. Then, prepare the cement mix according to the directions on the package and pour a 1-inch layer over the bottom of the larger box. Cover this concrete with wire mesh cut to the size of the box, then add an inch or two of concrete above it. Place the smaller box on top of the still-wet concrete and poke the dowels temporarily through the drainage holes and the concrete. Cut wire mesh to fit between the sides of the boxes, stand it on edge in the wet concrete already poured, then fill the space between the sides of the boxes with more concrete, covering the wire completely. After the cement has set for an hour or so, gently pull out the dowels. Let the concrete dry for a couple of days, then remove the forms, trim away excess concrete with a hammer and cold chisel, and ream out the drainage holes if necessary. In a few weeks, the planter will be ready for use.

BOXES AND TUBS

You can make or buy planters of virtually any size or shape. A large round planter is called a tub regardless of its composition; square and rectangular containers are always called boxes. Many designers prefer to use boxes for low, bushy plants but plant trees of any appreciable size in tubs.

Regardless of their shape, your containers should hold enough potting soil to protect the plants' roots from the ravages of cold, as nearly as possible the kind of protection they would get if they were in the earth. Plant roots are not nearly as hardy as their tops; saucer-magnolia branches, for example, will survive to 23° below zero, but their roots are killed at 23° above. In climates where the winter temperature falls just a few degrees below zero, a good rule of thumb is to allow a minimum of 14 inches of soil in all directions—depth, width and front-to-back—regardless of the size of the plant. In colder climates, even larger containers are needed for plants that spend the winter outdoors, and the perimeters of the containers should be lined with asbestos insulation. In moderate climates containers can be smaller.

A SOIL-MIX FORMULA

Soil for container plants should be rich. A good all-purpose formula is 2 parts garden loam or packaged potting soil to 1 part peat moss or leaf mold and 1 part builder's sand, perlite or vermiculite, with a tablespoonful of bone meal mixed in. Perlite and vermiculite are recommended for balconies and rooftops because they are very light. For good drainage, put an inch or more of gravel or cinders in the bottom of each pot and cover it with a thin layer of sphagnum moss or a piece of burlap, then add the soil mix.

A special but popular type of container is the strawberry jar, a juglike pot with openings in the sides where all manner of plants can be grown, including annuals, sedums and ivies as well as strawberry

Building and hanging a window box

Window boxes are not just for windows. These self-contained gardens work well in any place where space is scarce. They can be hooked onto a balcony railing with sturdy brackets or set directly on the floor of a porch or terrace to serve as out-of-ground flower beds.

Most garden centers sell ready-made window boxes, but many gardeners prefer to build their own to meet specific needs. A window box can easily be assembled with inch-thick boards cut to the desired dimensions and joined with brass screws. The wood should be rot-resistant cedar, redwood or cypress, treated with wood preservative for extra protection. Rustproof brass screws will hold much better than nails, which tend to work loose when soil in the box is watered.

The length of a window box should be no more than 3 feet; a longer box needs internal tie pieces to keep the sides from bulging. The width of the box depends on the number of plants it will hold. A box that is 8 inches wide will accommodate two rows of plants, one 11 inches wide three rows of plants. A depth of at least 7 or 8 inches is necessary to allow space for strong root development.

Once the boards have been cut, treat the wood, especially cut ends, with a copper-based preservative nontoxic to plants. Drill holes at the corners and along the sides, then screw the box together. Drill ½-inch drainage holes in a zigzag row every 5 or 6 inches along the bottom. If the box is to stand on the ground, nail several 1-inch wood strips across the bottom to raise it slightly so water can drain away.

If you paint the box, choose a light color that will absorb little heat. After the paint has dried, line the bottom of the box with fine aluminum screening, or cover the drainage holes with pottery shards and pour in a 2-inch layer of perlite; either of these measures will prevent the soil from washing out in a heavy rain. It will also slow the dripping when you water, especially important on the balcony or window sill of an apartment building where there are neighbors below.

Two metal window-box brackets, adjustable to support boxes from 8 to 11 inches wide, will hold a 3-foot-long box securely inside a railing or below a window sill. Window boxes are very heavy; make sure the brackets are solidly anchored to a structural part of the house, either a wall stud or the apron beneath a window sill. If you hook a box on a balcony railing, put it on the inside where it will be less hazardous if it should fall.

plants. After covering the jar's drainage hole with pottery shards, put in enough potting soil to reach the lowest side openings. Insert plants through these holes, cover the root balls with more soil, then place a cardboard tube down the center of the jar and fill in around it with soil to the next level of openings. Plant these openings, add more soil and continue until all the holes are planted and the soil is an inch from the top. Fill the tube with pebbles, then withdraw the tube gently, leaving the drainage column in place, and plant the top of the jar. Water plants in the jar through the drainage core.

Another special kind of container long popular in Europe, the window box, was in vogue in the United States in the first third of this century. It was used not only under windows but atop porch railings as well. Window boxes have become popular again, especially on the small balconies of apartments.

Fabricated boxes made of wood, plastic or metal can be purchased at most garden centers, or you can build your own *(page 97)*. The kind you choose will depend on where you plan to put them. Metal boxes, for instance, are not good if they face south or west; they can get so hot they will cook the plants. Avoid plastic boxes that have no provision for drainage. The two major criteria for window boxes are that they be strong enough to hold heavy, water-saturated soil and that they be securely fastened to the house or balcony railing. Unanchored boxes that are just set on window sills or railings are easily tipped. For safety's sake, window boxes should be supported by strong steel brackets.

WINDOW-BOX GARDENS   The planting possibilities for a window box are endless. Virtually anything will grow in one if it flourishes in your garden, so long as the plants selected have compatible needs for sunlight and soil. Depending on their branching patterns, plants should be set 5 to 8 inches apart, lined up in rows with 3 inches between rows. In a box 10 inches wide you might set ivy, lobelias or tuberous begonias in front, so they can cascade down the front of the box, some low-growing dwarf marigolds or petunias in the middle row and some taller flowers like geraniums in the rear. Or you might plant two or three varieties of the same flower, such as petunias, varying the color or shape, or combine flowers that share a certain color, such as blue trailing lobelias with blue stocks.

You may want to fill a window box with just one kind of unexpected flower. A London woman grew nothing but black-eyed Susans in her window box for many years and found that passersby were unfailingly delighted.

For more seasonal variety or for greater flexibility in choice of plants, you can set small potted plants in the box, rotating them in and out. The pots should stand atop a layer of perlite or gravel. They can be surrounded with sphagnum moss or vermiculite to give the box unity and to help the pots retain moisture.

A tray system will enable you to enjoy flowering bulbs in your window box. In the fall, plant hardy bulbs in a soil-filled metal tray about 4 inches deep and bury this container in the garden for the winter. (If you do not have a garden, refrigerate the tray for 12 to 16 weeks at about 40°.) In the spring, when shoots appear, move the tray to your window box and you soon will have a glorious display.

Plants in window boxes should be fertilized every week or so after the first month and, like hanging baskets, they usually need daily watering. In the fall, remove all of the soil and disinfect the box with 1 part household bleach to 9 parts water. During the winter you can fill the box with evergreen branches. In the spring, start over again with fresh soil.

Elsewhere in your container garden, in addition to discarding annuals and taking in house plants in the fall, you will want to condition the soil for any perennials, shrubs, trees and evergreens that will spend the winter outdoors. Build up a mulch of leaf mold or compost to a depth of 3 or 4 inches. Spray evergreen leaves and needles with an antidesiccant preparation to slow their rate of moisture loss. Water from time to time throughout the winter.

PREPARING FOR WINTER

In the spring, turn over the soil again and mix in more compost or leaf mold. Start a regular feeding regimen. This is also the time to move root-bound plants to larger containers. If you do not want a larger plant, you can prune the roots to slow the growth. Use a sharp spade to dig down around the edges of the container, and remove the outer 2 inches of soil in fistfuls, cutting off any roots that are encountered in the process. Fill the space with new soil, and prune the tree's branches somewhat to compensate for the root loss. Flowering or fruiting trees can be root pruned every two or three years, broad-leaved evergreens every three or four years, needled evergreens every three to five years. You may find it easier to prune half the roots in one year, pruning the rest the following season.

Throughout the growing months, keep grooming your plants. Prune to keep growth within bounds and to control the plants' shapes. Remove dead leaves and spent flowers. Wash the foliage regularly with a hose to dislodge insect pests and to remove soot and airborne chemicals. With such care, the plants in your container garden will thrive. And if one of your gardening friends chides you for not being a purist, pay no attention. You can change from a forest setting to a jungle atmosphere merely by shifting a few containers and baskets around. No backyard gardener can make that claim.

Portable plants from terrace to rooftop

Living areas that are set aside for outdoor entertaining and relaxation—a terrace or deck, or even a balcony—can be quickly dressed in style with flowering or foliage plants growing in handsome containers. Such plants can be functional as well as decorative. They can be positioned to ensure privacy; a few tub-grown evergreens may be enough to shield a patio from the eyes of passersby. Container-grown plants can provide shade; a leafy vine trained onto an arbor offers a pleasant shelter on a summer's day. Container plants can block a strong prevailing breeze, for the comfort of guests as well as for the protection of less rugged plants. They can even disguise architectural deficiencies—hiding a drainpipe or adding a lacy pattern to a dull, blank expanse of wall.

But the most important function of containerized plants—those grown outdoors in pots, tubs, urns, boxes and the like—is to establish an inviting environment that simply does not exist without them, carving out an intimate dining area, for example, or transforming a flat, featureless space into a terraced bank of flowers.

Portable containers accomplish more than simply giving quick color and greenery to barren areas. They provide mobility, enabling a gardener to shift plants from sun to shade and back again to match their light needs to the circling seasons. This mobility is an asset for a family on the move; plants in containers are easier to take along than those in the ground. Containers also make it possible to grow plants that could not survive the winter outdoors, since they can be moved indoors when frost threatens. And plants in containers make possible a continuous floral display; when spring bulbs have finished blooming, their containers can be moved out of the limelight to make way for others holding annuals that are just reaching their peak of glory.

Plants in containers are far from maintenance-free. Since they are constantly viewed from close-up, they need constant grooming so they always look their best. But most gardeners find the extra effort easy to take when it allows them to enjoy morning coffee or evening supper in an outdoor space as inviting as those on these pages.

Chrysanthemums, browallias and a Boston fern lead into a gazebo at the end of a garden path. The fall-blooming mums give way in spring to begonias and impatiens.

An invitation to the outdoors

The backyard terrace, that ubiquitous symbol of dedication to the pleasures of outdoor living, all too often sits in barren isolation, unloved and unused simply because it is uninviting. What is missing is the tie that binds house and terrace to the garden beyond. Nothing serves this need quite so well as plants in containers.

Such plants need to be selected with discrimination. Generally, they should be larger than house plants, to suit the larger scale of the world outdoors. They blend most comfortably if their foliage and flower colors bear a relationship to plants growing in the garden proper. And they should be displayed high as well as low; specimen plants hung from walls, eaves, trellises, even from nearby trees, add a dramatic dimension to the terrace landscape.

Dappled light, filtered through an eggcrate arbor, dictates the choice of shade-loving plants for this California terrace. Azaleas are used in spring, fuchsias during summer and the yellow and orange calendulas throughout winter. Fig trees and hanging baskets of Boston ferns add height to the design.

A sunny terrace facing south is adorned with chrysanthemums, petunias and gardenias that thrive in strong, direct sunlight. Ivy and lantana hang from the side of the house. A porch beyond the white doors shelters many of these plants in winter.

103

Plant decks, high and dry

The same qualities that make decks comfortable for people make them propitious places for plants in containers. Because a deck is raised off the ground, drainage and ventilation are superb. For the plants, these "comfort factors" mean less likelihood of disease and insect invasions, plus little danger that they will stand in soil so waterlogged that they drown.

Elevated decks do tend to be breezy, however. Plants subject to wind damage from dehydration need the protection of some sort of wind shield; some, such as ferns, require constantly moist soil and need frequent watering during dry periods. And tall plants need weight at their bases—either heavy pots or a potting mixture containing sand—to keep them from tipping over.

A wall of foliage around a hexagonal deck provides sufficient shelter from wind so a collection of wild bromeliads and palms can be displayed. Against the green backdrop, the brilliant colors of chrysanthemums and azaleas stand in sharp relief.

Like gigantic safety lights, two massive 17-inch pots of chrysanthemums mark the steps leading to a silvery deck made of Alaskan cedar. An arbor over the bar provides needed shade for ferns, spider plants, a wandering Jew and a tillandsia. It also supports a 50-year-old bougainvillea vine.

Gardens in the sky

Some of the world's most dedicated horticulturists live in harsh urban environments where they nurture exquisite gardens on balconies and rooftops. Pride in their achievement is justified: such gardening demands intensive care, right down to frequent rinsings to remove city grime from leaves. In a confined space flaws are magnified, so every plant must be pampered as a star performer.

A fifth-floor city balcony becomes an enchanting private bower with the addition of containers holding a towering azalea, pink cyclamens and impatiens. Telephone wires are masked with a fig tree (right) and an asparagus fern (left).

Nine varieties of petunias turn the roof of a city brownstone into a flowery retreat as accessible and inviting as any suburban backyard. The owners extended water and electricity lines to the roof. Then they carried 40 bags of potting soil weighing 40 pounds each up four flights of stairs.

A closer look at the garden opposite shows how the heavy baskets are placed where the walls of the building will support them. The squat containers give stability in wind. Vegetables—lettuce, tomatoes and cucumbers—are grown in other containers.

COLOR

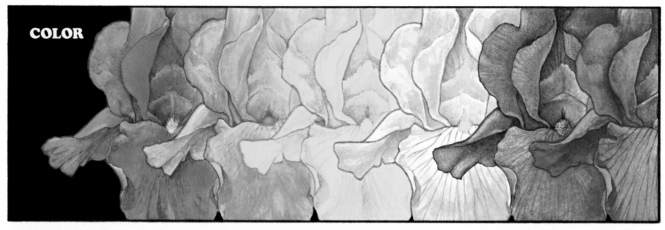

SHAPE

TEXTURE

PATTERN

An encyclopedia of decorative plant materials 5

Plants and plant materials commonly available and widely used in decorating home interiors are grouped according to their primary visual characteristics on the encyclopedia pages that follow. The four major categories used—color, shape, texture and pattern—are those that professional decorators and arrangers consider most important in determining how to integrate any particular plant into the decorating scheme of a room.

To make use of this encyclopedia, you should think of plants as raw materials for decorating, choosing them with the care you would give to selecting fabric for a sofa, or a patterned rug to complement that fabric. There is room for imagination but little room for compromise in this approach; nothing will do but the best you can find to fulfill the decorating need you have in mind.

You can use this encyclopedia as a specific guide to find the exact plant you need, but you should bear in mind that each plant shown is merely a stand-in for countless others that display the same visual characteristics. In all, 171 plants and plant materials are illustrated and described from a decorator's viewpoint. If you need a striking sculptural plant to give a room a major point of interest, you will not only find several suggested but information on what kind of care they require. If your color scheme demands blue flowers, which are not at all common, you will find them here with advice on how to handle them to lengthen their life as cut flowers, and even how to dry those that will retain their blue color for months.

But of greater importance is the fact that evaluating plants and flowers for their decorative value requires a special way of seeing. Some colors are brash and demanding; others cool and subtle. Some shapes are delicate and lacy, others bold and even repulsive, if nature has provided weapons to repel that plant's enemies. But a discriminating search will reveal many plants that can play a vital, living role as part of a home's essential character.

A rainbow of irises, the fanciful shape of a blue and orange bird-of-paradise, the rough texture of a purple sea holly and the playful spots of a hybrid lily illustrate the visual groupings in this encyclopedia.

COLORS: Green

When dealing with plants, amateur arrangers and decorators often regard green as a neutral backdrop. Those with more experience know that it is a strong color in its own right. Shades of green can be blended to create quiet, restful bouquets. Greens also serve to unify blues and yellows and contrast crisply with complementary reds.

HEART-LEAVED PHILODENDRON
Philodendron oxycardium
Leaf size: 2 to 4 inches

SPEAR-LEAVED FERN
Doryopteris pedata palmata
Plant height: 1 to 1½ feet

RUDOLPH ROEHRS DIEFFENBACHIA
Dieffenbachia picta
Plant height: to 5 feet

CUSHION SPURGE
Euphorbia epithymoides
Cutting length: to 1 foot

INDOOR OAK
Nicodemia diversifolia
Plant height: 1 to 1½ feet

FLOWERING TOBACCO
Nicotiana alata grandiflora
Plant height: 8 to 18 inches
Flower diameter: 2 inches

PANDA PLANT
Kalanchoe tomentosa
Plant height: 6 to 8 inches

TANYOSHO PINE
Pinus densiflora umbraculifera
Needle length: 2 to 5 inches

BELLS-OF-IRELAND
Moluccella laevis
Cutting length: to 3 feet

BUTTON FERN
Pellaea rotundifolia
Frond length: 18 inches

BELLS-OF-IRELAND. Gracefully curved spikes of green bells-of-Ireland last one to two weeks in bouquets if they are cut when the tiny florets inside the upper bells are fresh, then left standing overnight in water in a cool place. To accentuate curves, stand the plants in ice water for two hours, then move to warm water. Cut in fall when silvery gray, bells-of-Ireland dry readily hung upside down in a dark, airy place. To keep the summer color, cut when they are green and dry for one and one half days in silica gel.

CUSHION SPURGE. Cut half-opened clusters of cushion spurge in late spring and early summer; they last up to a week in water if stem ends are dipped in boiling water, then allowed to stand overnight in water in a cool place.

DIEFFENBACHIA. Erect plants that have broad, often patterned leaves, dieffenbachias are durable house plants. They can be maintained in low light but they grow best in bright indirect light. As plants mature, lower leaves drop; to keep them low and shrubby, cut stalks back each spring.

FERN, BUTTON. Oval ½-inch leaflets that seem polished crowd along the button fern's stiff, glossy stalks. Young red leaflets add a touch of color. Start small button ferns in pots or open terrariums where they receive bright indirect light; let the 18-inch fronds of mature plants trail from baskets. These ferns can be moved onto a shady terrace when night temperatures stay above 50°.

FERN, SPEAR-LEAVED. Bearing distinctly different sterile and fertile fronds, the spear-leaved fern is a handsome house plant. Short-stemmed sterile fronds resemble maple leaves, while the longer fertile fronds are cut into leaflets. Fronds turn a darker green as they mature. Place these plants where they will have bright indirect sunlight, night temperatures of 60° to 70° and at least 60 per cent humidity.

FLOWERING TOBACCO. Flowering tobacco, a fragrant summer-blooming annual, has dwarf varieties only 8 to 10 inches tall that can be grown in pots. Give them four hours of direct sunlight daily. For cutting, choose clusters with few open flowers and stand overnight in water in a cool place. Clusters last up to a week as buds open successively.

INDOOR OAK. The shape of its 1- to 2-inch iridescent leaves gives the indoor oak its common name. With four hours of direct sunlight daily and temperatures from 65° at night to 85° by day, the plant grows to 18 inches. Keep it bushy by pinching off new growth.

PANDA PLANT. Soft-looking panda plants have succulent leaves edged with brown. Plant them in dish gardens or arrange them on window sills or tables where they will receive at least four hours of direct sunlight daily and night temperatures are 50° or more.

PHILODENDRON, HEART-LEAVED. You can grow the familiar heart-leaved philodendron as a trailing plant or train its stem around a support. These plants grow best in bright indirect sunlight and are easily maintained. Used in arrangements, philodendron stems may root and grow in water.

PINE, TANYOSHO. Aromatic pine boughs last for weeks, sometimes months, in water. Wash branches, slash stem ends a few times 3 inches deep and stand overnight in water. When arranging, remove all needles below the water line.

Conditioning plant materials, page 58; drying plant materials, page 67.

Yellow

A bowl of yellow narcissus in midwinter bloom suggests spring sunshine on even the drabbest day. Yellow is the color closest to white in its ability to reflect light. It is a vibrant, highly visible color. Use yellow to balance weighty dark blues and purples, to accent blues and greens, to warm dull browns and tans, and to add brightness when red or orange would seem too hot.

FERN-LEAVED YARROW
Achillea filipendulina
Cutting length: to 4½ feet
Flower cluster diameter: 3 to 6 inches

COMMON NASTURTIUM
Tropaeolum majus
Flower diameter: 2 inches

COREOPSIS
Coreopsis species
Cutting length: 5 inches to 3 feet
Flower diameter: 1 to 2 inches

CALIFORNIA GOLDENROD
Solidago species and hybrids
Cutting length: 2 to 9 feet

DAY LILY
Hemerocallis hybrids
Cutting length: 15 inches to 4 feet
Flower diameter: 3 to 8 inches

SMALL-CUPPED DAFFODIL
Narcissus species
Plant height: 3 inches to 2 feet
Flower diameter: 1 to 3 inches

BORDER FORSYTHIA
Forsythia intermedia
Cutting length: to 8 feet

MARIGOLD
Tagetes species
Plant height: 6 inches to 3 feet
Flower diameter: 1 to 5 inches

COREOPSIS. Cut daisy-like coreopsis blossoms in the summer when their petals have just opened, stand them in warm water and leave overnight. Cut flowers will last from one to two weeks. Or dry mature coreopsis blossoms face up in silica gel for two days.

DAFFODIL. Dispel winter drabness with bright daffodils planted in pots at intervals so that they will bloom all winter long. Flowers on potted bulbs last longest if they are given indirect light and temperatures below 68°. Outdoor flowers, cut just as they open in spring, will last five days. Split the stem ends of the flowers and dip them in hot water, then stand them overnight in water that reaches 4 inches above the split. Dry these delicate flowers in silica gel. Cut stems off below the cups, replace stems with wires and dry for about two days.

DAY LILY. Although individual blooms last but a day, each day-lily flower stalk bears several blossoms that open successively. Cut stalks with well-developed buds, stand them in warm water and leave overnight. To keep flowers open in the evening, refrigerate during the day. Day-lily blossoms dry in one day in silica gel, with yellow and orange turning bronze or brown.

FORSYTHIA. Cut arching sprays of forsythia with closed buds from January through March to force the flowers into early indoor bloom. Flowers appear before the leaves and last about a week. To arrange, remove lower twigs, split stem ends and peel bark back 3 inches. Immerse in warm water and leave overnight before bending branches into shape. Flowering branches can be cut and preserved with glycerin, but the flowers turn brown.

GOLDENROD. Gather sprays of goldenrod in summer and fall, choosing those with just-opened flowers with a few green buds. Remove the leaves below the water line and change the water daily to make blooms last one to three weeks. To dry, hang erect types of goldenrod upside down or stand trailing kinds in a container for a week, or bury either type in silica gel for two days.

MARIGOLD. Given a sunny location, pots of marigolds will decorate outdoor living spaces with an abundance of blossoms from summer through fall. Cut marigolds will last one to two weeks. Pick varieties with a single layer of petals when barely open, those with double layers when three-quarters open: stand them in warm water and leave overnight. To dry, strip off leaves and hang upside down for two weeks. To preserve better color, cut off stems, replace the stems with florist's wires and dry the flower heads in silica gel for four to five days.

NASTURTIUM. For flowers that bloom on the terrace from early spring through summer, grow pots of nasturtiums in full or filtered sunlight. When cut, fully opened flowers last three to five days and long-stemmed leaves last up to two weeks. Recut and split stems, place in warm water and leave overnight. The flowers will turn toward the light.

YARROW. Cut yarrow flowers in summer when half of the blossoms in a cluster are open, stand them in warm water and leave overnight. Flowers last from three days to two weeks, depending on the variety. To dry, cut fully opened flowers and hang upside down for about two weeks. Dry the fernlike leaves on a flat surface.

Conditioning plant materials, page 58; forcing branches, page 71; preserving in glycerin, page 70; drying plant materials, page 67. 115

Orange

A color that compels attention, orange combines the warmth of red with the liveliness of yellow. You can blend it harmoniously with either, or accent dull beiges and browns with its fire, or pair it with blues and purples to underscore their coolness. Orange is at its best in natural lights; under artificial illumination it may become garish.

TITHONIA
Tithonia rotundifolia
Cutting length: to 4 feet
Flower diameter: 3 inches

ORANGE STREPTOSOLEN
Streptosolen jamesonii
Flower diameter: 1 inch

CALAMONDIN ORANGE
Citrus mitis
Plant height: to 2 feet
Fruit diameter: 1 to 2 inches

LALAND FIRE THORN
Pyracantha coccinea lalandei
Berry diameter: ¼ inch

CALENDULA
Calendula officinalis
Cutting length: to 2 feet
Flower diameter: 2 to 4 inches

BUTTERFLY WEED
Asclepias tuberosa
Cutting length: to 2 feet
Flower cluster diameter: 2 inches

116

CHINESE LANTERN PLANT
Physalis alkekengi
Cutting length: to 2 feet
Pod length: 2 inches

BLACK-EYED-SUSAN VINE
Thunbergia alata
Stem length: 2 to 4 feet
Flower diameter: 1 to 2 inches

BLACK-EYED-SUSAN VINE. Cascading from a basket or climbing a small trellis, the black-eyed-Susan vine's paper-like flowers and spear-shaped leaves are decorative indoors or out. Give indoor plants at least four hours of direct sunlight daily; outdoor plants require full sun and night temperatures above 50°. Use flowering stems in arrangements after standing them overnight in water.

BUTTERFLY WEED. Cut brilliant clusters of butterfly-weed blossoms from midsummer to early fall when they are half to three quarters open. Dip stem ends in boiling water and stand them overnight in water. Butterfly-weed flowers dry in silica gel in one and a half days. Cut the canoe-shaped seed pods while they are still green; hung upside down, they will dry to beige.

CALENDULA. Summer-blooming calendulas last a week or more in water. Cut the flowers when they are three quarters open and stand them overnight in water. Recut the stems under water before arranging. Each day recut stems and change water to prevent decay. To dry, clip off the stem, push florist's wire through the flower head, and dry face up in silica gel for up to three days.

CHINESE LANTERN PLANT. Floral decorators covet the dried orange seed pods of the Chinese lantern plant. Cut stems in fall just after the papery lanterns turn orange. Strip off leaves and stand stems in a container without water; let them dry in a cool, airy place for two weeks. Split some of the pods open along the veins before drying to achieve curling shapes. Spray the pods with hair lacquer after they are dry. Use stems with green seed pods in fresh arrangements after standing them in water overnight.

FIRE THORN. Cut branches of fire thorn (pyracantha) year round. The tiny white blooms of spring develop into red or orange berries by fall. Condition cut branches by splitting stem ends vertically two or three times 3 inches deep, then stand them overnight in water. Clip thorns for easier handling. Leafy or berried branches can be preserved with glycerin; the berry color fades slightly. Spray treated berries with hair lacquer.

ORANGE, CALAMONDIN. Providing months of brightly colored fruits, calamondin orange plants with shiny evergreen leaves can be grown as house plants in the north or outdoors in climates where night temperatures do not drop below 50°. These citrus plants produce fragrant blossoms in spring and fall, followed by oranges that are about 1 inch in diameter. Give house plants at least four hours of direct sunlight daily. Plants can be pruned to maintain the desired shape and size. Cuttings can be used in arrangements if the woody stems are split and left standing overnight in water.

STREPTOSOLEN. Orange streptosolen is treasured as a house plant because it blooms through the winter and intermittently at other times. Plants can be trained with stakes into treelike shapes up to 3 feet tall or allowed to tumble from hanging containers. They need four hours of direct sunlight in winter and bright indirect sunlight in summer.

TITHONIA. Tall-stemmed, daisy-like tithonias last up to a week in summer bouquets. Cut either buds or open blossoms that have tight centers. Strip off the lower leaves and stand overnight in water. In the fall, pick stems with seed heads and hang them upside down to dry for two weeks.

Conditioning plant materials, page 58; drying plant materials, page 67; preserving in glycerin, page 70.

Red

The strength of the color red is such that one red rose can have as much impact as an entire bouquet of less dramatic hues. Many people find pure reds objectionable in large quantities. Use this overpowering color with discretion as a dominant hue. Red cools and becomes more formal as the color shifts toward purple and becomes brighter on the orange side.

CYCLAMEN
Cyclamen persicum
Plant height: 8 to 14 inches
Flower diameter: 2 to 3 inches

PARROT TULIP
Tulipa hybrids
Plant height: 9 to 30 inches
Flower diameter: 1 to 7 inches

ENGLISH HOLLY
Ilex aquifolium
Berry diameter: ¼ inch

ROSE
Hybrid tea varieties
Cutting length: to 20 inches
Flower diameter: 3 to 8 inches

IMPATIENS
Impatiens wallerana
Plant height: 6 inches to 2 feet
Flower diameter: 1 to 2½ inches

CARNATION
Dianthus caryophyllus
Cutting length: 1½ to 3 feet
Flower diameter: 1 to 3 inches

AMARYLLIS
Hippeastrum hybrid
Plant height: 1½ to 2 feet
Flower diameter: to 10 inches

COMMON GERANIUM
Pelargonium hortorum
Plant height: 3 inches to 3 feet
Flower cluster diameter: to 4 inches

AMARYLLIS. Planted in pots in the fall, amaryllis bulbs send forth clusters of spectacular lily-like blossoms from January through April. These huge blooms last up to seven days in bright indirect sunlight with night temperatures of 60° to 65°. The flowers are not usually cut, but they can be cut and conditioned by standing them overnight in warm water. Recut stems under water just before arranging.

CARNATION. Garden carnations picked in summer will last up to 10 days. Stand them in warm water, leave overnight, then recut the stems under water just before arranging. For drying, choose barely open flowers. Cut off each stem 1½ inches below the flower head, replace the stem with wire, and bury it face up in silica gel for two or three days.

CYCLAMEN. In fall, buy cyclamens in flower or plant tubers in pots for winter and spring bloom indoors. Cyclamens grow best in indirect light with temperatures ranging from a cool 40° at night to 65° by day. Cyclamen flowers last up to three months on plants. Though cyclamens are not commonly arranged, they can be if fully opened flowers and leaves are pulled cleanly from the tuber. Recut and split the stems, then stand them in water overnight before arranging. The blooms will last five to eight days.

GERANIUM. Grown in full sun on a terrace, pots or hanging baskets of geraniums provide color from summer through fall. Or grow them indoors for flowers from winter through fall, providing at least four hours of direct sunlight daily and night temperatures of 50° to 55°. For cut flowers that last up to eight days, cut clusters when half the buds have opened, remove foliage and split stem ends. Stand the flowers in warm water and leave overnight before arranging.

HOLLY. Branches of holly with bright red berries and dark green glossy leaves last a month or more in water, indefinitely when dried or treated with a preservative. Cut branches in the early fall, slash stem ends vertically three or four times about 3 inches deep, then stand overnight in water. To preserve holly foliage for many months, stand the branches in a glycerin solution.

IMPATIENS. In sunny or shady window boxes, hanging baskets or patio tubs, impatiens will bloom from summer through fall. For year-round color, grow them in bright indirect light in temperatures from 60° at night to 70° or more by day. Pinch off stem tips to create bushier plants.

ROSE. Cut tight rosebuds from summer to fall and plunge the stems immediately into tepid water containing a preservative. Stand the container in a cool place for at least one hour. Just before arranging, cut off unwanted foliage and thorns, then trim a fraction of an inch from each stem end. The blooms will stay fresh up to a week. To dry, remove thorns and foliage and bury the flower and its stem horizontally in silica gel. Allow one and one half days for fully opened flowers, two and one half days or more for buds.

TULIP. Spring-blooming outdoors, tulip bulbs can be grown in pots for indoor blooms from winter through spring. Tulips last up to 10 days on indoor plants in indirect light if temperatures range from 40° at night to 68° by day. For cutting, choose buds, wrap them individually in wet newspaper and stand overnight in water. To use tulips in arrangements, run wires through their stems to prevent the flowers from turning toward the light.

Conditioning plant materials, page 58; drying plant materials, page 67; preserving in glycerin, page 70.

Purple

*Some flower arrangers shun purple as dark and receding.
This meld of blue and red can indeed be somber, but its reddish
shades, long the symbol of wealth and royalty, are elegant.
Bluish purples are emphatic, but violet tints of those hues
become delicate. Purple can be used to unify reds and blues;
its coolness is intensified when it is paired with orange.*

HYACINTH
Hyacinthus species
Flower spike height: 6 to 10 inches

COMMON LILAC
Syringa vulgaris
Flower cluster length: 6 to 8 inches

AFRICAN VIOLET
Saintpaulia ionantha
Plant height: 4 to 6 inches
Flower diameter: 1 to 2 inches

CROCUS
Crocus hybrids
Plant height: 4 to 6 inches
Flower diameter: 1 to 2 inches

PURPLE HEART
Setcreasea purpurea
Leaf length: 5 to 7 inches

GLOXINIA
Sinningia speciosa
Plant height: 1 foot
Flower diameter: 3 to 6 inches

ASTER
Aster species and hybrids
Cutting length: 9 inches to 3 feet
Flower diameter: 2½ inches

PETUNIA
Petunia hybrids
Plant height: 6 to 18 inches
Flower diameter: 2 to 7 inches

AFRICAN VIOLET. The African violet maintains its status as the favorite house plant by blooming abundantly year round if it is displayed in bright but indirect sunlight. Just-opened flowers, unusual and dainty as cut blooms, last up to a week in arrangements if the stems are recut under water and left standing in water overnight. The leaves, which frequently root in water, can be conditioned the same way. Brush the backs of the flowers where petals join with a 50-50 mixture of egg white and water to retard petal fall.

ASTER. Clusters of wiry-stemmed perennial asters last up to two weeks in arrangements. Different varieties bloom in spring, summer or fall. Cut the clusters when three quarters of their flowers are open. Recut the stems under water and stand them in water overnight before arranging. If stems are woody, split an inch or so of the ends. To dry, push florist's wire through each flower head and dry face up in silica gel for one and one half days.

CROCUS. Satiny blossoms of potted crocus, rising amid grasslike leaves, bring a touch of spring to a wintry room. Place these plants where they will get four hours of direct sunlight daily, night temperatures around 40° and day temperatures of 68° or lower. For cut flowers that will last four to six days, pick stems with nearly open cups and stand them overnight in water.

GLOXINIA. Velvety gloxinia bells nodding above compact rosettes of hairy, oval leaves bloom in succession for two to four weeks at intervals throughout the year, followed by periods of rest. You can grow or purchase different varieties to achieve a succession of blooms. Give the plants bright indirect sunlight.

HYACINTH. Sweetly perfumed hyacinths can be purchased as blooming plants in winter. Place them in indirect sunlight where temperatures are 40° to 45° at night and 60° or lower by day. Flowers cut in the spring garden last three to six days. Cut fully open spikes above the white portion of the stem, split the stem end and stand overnight in water.

LILAC. Forced into early bloom or cut while in flower, fragrant lilacs last a week in water. Branches cut in early spring bloom indoors in four to five weeks. Cut the flowers in late spring when clusters are one quarter to half open. Remove leaves, split stem ends, peel bark back 3 inches, and stand in water overnight or until clusters are open. Condition nonflowering branches for foliage. To dry, lay clusters horizontally in silica gel for one and one half days.

PETUNIA. Petunias planted in containers and placed in sunny locations provide outdoor color from spring to fall if they are pinched back to form mounds and to prevent seed from developing. Cut these plants back in fall and move them indoors, placing them where they will receive at least four hours of direct sunlight daily. Or start seeds in midsummer for new winter plants. Fully open double petunias are best for cutting. Although the blooms collapse when cut, they revive when conditioned overnight in water containing a commercial preservative. Arrange in plain water, removing foliage to prevent decay. Flowers last four to seven days.

PURPLE HEART. Named for the color of its leaves, purple heart is often displayed cascading from hanging baskets. Plants thrive with four hours of direct sunlight daily but can be maintained in bright indirect light.

Conditioning plant materials, page 58; drying plant materials, page 67; forcing branches, page 71.

Blue

True blue is so rare in horticulture that gardeners often call flowers blue when they are actually violet, mauve or some other related hue. But cool blues do exist. Blues such as those illustrated harmonize subtly with foliage greens, creating a sense of spaciousness. And they blend into quiet settings that stronger colors might overwhelm.

GRAPE HYACINTH
Muscari armeniacum
Plant height: 9 to 12 inches
Flower spike height: 1 to 3 inches

DUTCH IRIS
Iris hybrids and species
Cutting length: 3 inches to 3½ feet
Flower diameter: 1½ to 10 inches

BLUE MARGUERITE
Felicia amelloides
Plant height: 1 foot
Flower diameter: 1 to 1½ inches

BLUE LACE FLOWER
Trachymene caerulea
Cutting length: to 2½ feet
Flower cluster diameter: 2 to 3 inches

COMMON BIGLEAF HYDRANGEA
Hydrangea macrophylla
Cutting length: to 6 feet
Flower cluster diameter: 8 to 15 inches

CORNFLOWER
Centaurea cyanus
Plant height: 10 inches to 3 feet
Flower diameter: 1 to 2 inches

CANDLE DELPHINIUM
Delphinium elatum hybrids
Cutting length: to 6 feet

CINERARIA
Senecio cruentus
Plant height: 8 inches to 1½ feet
Flower diameter: 1 to 4 inches

BLUE LACE FLOWER. Resembling wild Queen Anne's lace, the blue lace flower can be grown indoors where it gets four hours of direct sunlight daily. The umbrella-shaped flower clusters last a week or more in arrangements if they are cut when half the buds are still closed. Stand the wiry stems in water overnight. Flower heads will dry in one and one half days in silica gel but they may wilt later.

BLUE MARGUERITE. Daisy-like blue marguerites bloom almost continuously indoors if they are given at least four hours of direct sunlight daily. To arrange flowers cut in the garden, strip foliage, place stems in warm water to start, and refrigerate overnight. Blossoms sometimes close at night.

CINERARIA. During winter and spring, potted cineraria plants available at florist shops bear clusters of daisy-like flowers. Place the pots in bright indirect sunlight where nights are 40° to 45° and days are 68° or lower. For cut flowers that will last up to a week, cut cinerarias when three fourths of the flowers in a cluster are open; stand them overnight in water.

CORNFLOWER. Cheerful, ragged cornflower blossoms add an old-fashioned charm to fresh bouquets, where they last up to a week. Cut fully open blooms in summer and stand them overnight in water. These flowers fade when they are hung in bunches to dry. To get brightly colored dried cornflowers, dry the flower heads face up in silica gel for one and one half to two days after hooking a wire stem through each one.

DELPHINIUM. Tall, graceful delphinium wands add an elegant touch to flower arrangements. Buy them in winter or cut them in the garden from late spring through summer. Cut spikes that have half of the buds closed, remove bottom leaves and side shoots, then stand them overnight in water. As the individual florets gradually open over a week, remove the faded lower blossoms. Delphiniums can be hung upside down to dry, but they dry better if placed horizontally in silica gel, with stems attached, for two to three days.

GRAPE HYACINTH. The conical blooms of grape hyacinths add fragrance as well as color to winter rooms. Buy plants in bloom and provide four hours of direct sunlight daily, night temperatures of 40° to 45° and days of 68° or lower. Or cut spikes in the spring garden when one fourth to one half of the florets are open. Flowers will last up to six days if you split an inch of the stem ends and stand them overnight in water. You can dry grape hyacinths standing in a dry vase, or dry them in two days in silica gel.

HYDRANGEA, BIGLEAF. Purchased as blooming house plants, hydrangeas seem to fill a room with their soft, enormous blue spheres. Give plants bright indirect sunlight. Or cut flowers from outdoor shrubs in summer when half the buds are open. Sear stem ends and stand them overnight in water. Flowers last a week. Older blooms dry best; cut them after petals become papery and dry by standing them in a dry vase, or hang them upside down. For more vivid color, dry head down in silica gel for one and one half days.

IRIS. Flanked by swordlike leaves, irises last a week to ten days in fresh bouquets. Buy stalks in winter or cut in the garden when the first buds unroll in spring and early summer. Stand flowers and leaves overnight in separate containers of water. In the arrangement, snip faded lower blossoms as upper ones open. Pick seed pods in fall.

Conditioning plant materials, page 58; drying plant materials, page 67.

White

Far from being colorless, white actually is created by combining all the colors in a ray of light. White is the safest color in decorating, a perfect neutral, able to blend comfortably with any other color. Use substantial quantities of white to achieve maximum brightness, smaller amounts if you are seeking contrast or highlights.

FLOWERING DOGWOOD
Cornus florida
Flower diameter: 3 to 5 inches

SHASTA DAISY
Chrysanthemum maximum
Cutting length: 1 to 3 feet
Flower diameter: 3 to 6 inches

LILY OF THE VALLEY
Convallaria majalis
Cutting length: 6 to 8 inches
Flower diameter: ¼ inch

CATTLEYA ORCHID
Cattleya species and hybrids
Flower diameter: 3 to 8 inches

CALADIUM
Caladium hortulanum
Plant height: 1 to 3 feet
Leaf length: 6 inches to 2 feet

GARDENIA
Gardenia jasminoides veitchii
Plant height: 1 to 3 feet
Flower diameter: 3 to 5 inches

NATAL PLUM
Carissa grandiflora
Plant height: 1 to 1½ feet
Flower diameter: 1½ to 2 inches

EASTER LILY
Lilium longiflorum
Plant height: 1 to 3 feet
Flower diameter: 4 to 5 inches

CALADIUM. The massive leaves of caladiums provide effective white accents on plants growing outdoors in summer in partial shade, or indoors in bright indirect sunlight. Leaves wither during a plant's five-month dormant period. Buy new plants to achieve a year-round display. For cut foliage that will last up to two weeks, split stem ends and stand the leaves upright in water overnight.

DOGWOOD, FLOWERING. To force dogwood branches into early bloom in two to four weeks, cut them in spring as soon as buds swell, split stem ends, peel bark back 2 inches, and immerse in water for 24 hours. Then stand stem ends in water in a cool place until buds open. Flowers last a week or more. Cut branches in summer for their green foliage and in fall for red leaves and berries. Bare winter boughs also make striking arrangements. Preserve foliage with glycerin, or dry individual flowers in silica gel for one and one half days.

GARDENIA. Creamy gardenia blooms surrounded by waxy evergreen leaves bloom outdoors on sunny patios in late spring and early summer. Indoors, they bloom in a location with at least four hours of direct sunlight daily, night temperatures of 60° to 65° and day temperatures of 70°, with at least 50 per cent humidity. Cut flowering branches for arrangements, split stem ends and stand them overnight in water. To condition flowers only, place their short stems on wet cotton and refrigerate them overnight.

LILY, EASTER. Widely available as flowering potted plants in spring, trumpet-shaped Easter lilies last up to a week indoors in bright indirect light, with temperatures from 40° at night to 68° by day. Cut garden-grown Easter lilies in summer, choosing stalks with barely open blooms. Split the stem ends and stand overnight in water.

LILY OF THE VALLEY. Delicately perfumed lilies of the valley last up to a week as cut flowers. In late spring, cut stems with one fourth of the buds open and stand overnight in warm water. Dry lilies of the valley one and one half days in silica gel. Preserve leaves by submerging them in a 50-50 solution of glycerin and water.

NATAL PLUM. A low-growing evergreen, Natal plum produces fragrant white flowers amid closely packed oval leaves at intervals year round; it also bears plum-shaped red fruit. Pots can be moved outdoors during spring and summer into either sun or shade when night temperatures are above 50°. Indoors, give them at least four hours of direct sunlight daily.

ORCHID, CATTLEYA. Potted cattleya orchids provide up to six weeks of blooms at intervals year round, provided they are given four or more hours of direct sunlight daily, temperatures from 55° at night to 68° by day, and 50 per cent humidity. For corsages or arrangements, cut fully opened flowers, trim the orchid's stem end on a slant and either wrap it with wet cotton or place it in a tiny water vial. Cut flowers last four days if refrigerated when not on display.

SHASTA DAISY (CHRYSANTHEMUM). Perennial chrysanthemums like the Shasta daisy offer a great array of sizes and textures. Place potted plants where they will get at least four hours of direct sunlight daily. Cut garden mums from late summer through fall; flowers last up to three weeks. If stems are woody, split ends before standing in water overnight. Recut stems under water and remove leaves below the water line.

Conditioning plant materials, page 58; forcing branches, page 71; preserving in glycerin, page 70; drying plant materials, page 67.

SHAPES: Bold

Few people can walk past the huge, deeply indented leaves of a monstera plant without looking twice at the striking shapes. Decorators use such boldly shaped plants to focus attention on some particular aspect of a room. Similarly, an arranger needs only one or two bold blossoms of a sunflower or calla lily to give a crowning touch to an important arrangement.

SCHEFFLERA
Brassaia actinophylla
Plant height: to 8 feet

JAPANESE FATSIA
Fatsia japonica
Plant height: to 4 feet

MONSTERA
Monstera deliciosa
Leaf diameter: 8 to 12 inches

COMMON SUNFLOWER
Helianthus annuus
Flower diameter: 8 to 14 inches

CALLA LILY
Zantedeschia species
Cutting length: 1½ to 4 feet
Flower size: 4 to 8 inches

BIRD-OF-PARADISE
Strelitzia reginae
Plant height: 2 to 4 feet
Flower size: 6 inches

TAILFLOWER
Anthurium andreanum
Plant height: 2 to 3 feet
Bract length: 3 to 6 inches

WENDLAND'S PHILODENDRON
Philodendron wendlandii
Leaf length: 1 to 1½ feet

SADDLE-LEAVED PHILODENDRON
Philodendron selloum
Plant height: to 4 feet

BIRD-OF-PARADISE. Multicolored petals fan out like brilliant plumage from the boat-shaped bract that grows horizontally from the tip of each bird-of-paradise flower stalk. Potted plants usually bloom in summer and fall; they need at least four hours of direct sunlight daily and night temperatures of 50° to 55°. As cut flowers, blooms last up to two weeks if they first stand overnight in water. Cut stems at an angle with a sharp knife. As each flower fades, remove it and gently lift the one below out of its bract. Bird-of-paradise can be dried standing in a dry vase, but the flowers quickly lose their vivid color.

CALLA LILY. Waxy calla-lily funnels appear at intervals year round when potted bulbs are grown in bright indirect sunlight with night temperatures of 50° to 65°. You can also buy the fragrant blooms year round or cut them in the garden in spring and early summer. Open flowers last a week or more, buds and leaves up to three weeks. Prick the lower stems in several spots and stand overnight in water.

FATSIA, JAPANESE. With deeply cut, shiny, hand-shaped leaves up to 16 inches across, a massive Japanese fatsia grandly fills a large space. Plants prefer at least four hours of direct sunlight daily and temperatures of 40° to 55° at night, 65° or lower by day, but they survive in bright indirect light.

MONSTERA. A climbing jungle vine, monstera thrives in almost any light or temperature range. Its light-green young philodendron-like leaves soon become dark green and leathery, perforated with holes and split deeply along the edges. Given supports, monsteras grow to ceiling height. The leaves will root in water and can be used in large arrangements.

PHILODENDRON, SADDLE-LEAVED. Deep indentations with rippled edges turn the enormous leaves of the saddle-leaved philodendron into leathery lace. These durable plants form clumps up to 6 feet across. You can grow them in bright indirect sunlight, but the stronger the light, the larger the leaves will be. Treated with glycerin, the foliage lasts indefinitely, making it useful for large arrangements.

PHILODENDRON, WENDLAND'S. Since its long, broad leaves grow in clumps rather than on vines as do many other philodendrons, Wendland's philodendron needs no support. This large, low-growing philodendron should be given room to spread in a location with bright indirect light.

SCHEFFLERA. Like glossy umbrellas, clusters of leathery, elliptical leaflets top the stiff canes of schefflera plants. A schefflera will thrive in indirect light. To control its height and shape, snip off new growth just above a leaflet cluster.

SUNFLOWER. The coarse blossoms of annual sunflowers have rugged, pebbly centers, providing texture as well as color in large summer arrangements. Cut fully open flowers that still have tight centers. Strip off the lower leaves, run florist's wire up the center of each stem to support the heavy heads and stand overnight in water. The flowers last a week or more. Let seed heads dry on plants or hang them upside down indoors to dry for winter bouquets.

TAILFLOWER. Exotic tailflowers are dramatic as house plants or in arrangements. Glossy, heart-shaped, brightly colored bracts appear continuously on plants in bright indirect light. Flowers last a month on plants. Cut, they last for two or three weeks if first placed in water overnight.

Conditioning plant materials, page 58; drying plant materials, page 67; preserving in glycerin, page 70.

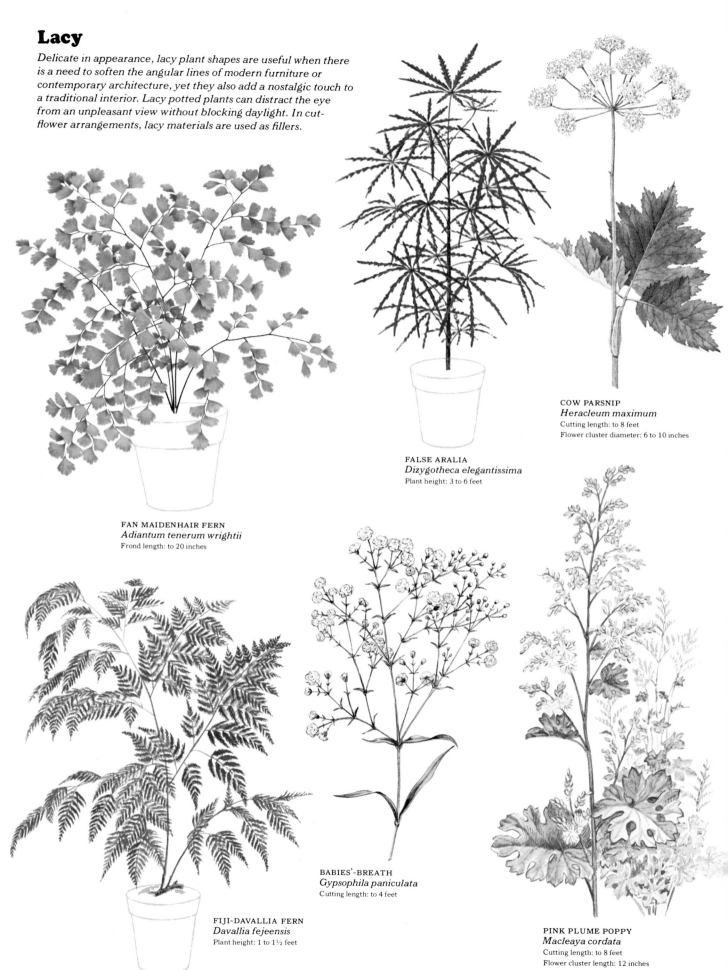

Lacy

Delicate in appearance, lacy plant shapes are useful when there is a need to soften the angular lines of modern furniture or contemporary architecture, yet they also add a nostalgic touch to a traditional interior. Lacy potted plants can distract the eye from an unpleasant view without blocking daylight. In cut-flower arrangements, lacy materials are used as fillers.

COW PARSNIP
Heracleum maximum
Cutting length: to 8 feet
Flower cluster diameter: 6 to 10 inches

FALSE ARALIA
Dizygotheca elegantissima
Plant height: 3 to 6 feet

FAN MAIDENHAIR FERN
Adiantum tenerum wrightii
Frond length: to 20 inches

BABIES'-BREATH
Gypsophila paniculata
Cutting length: to 4 feet

FIJI-DAVALLIA FERN
Davallia fejeensis
Plant height: 1 to 1½ feet

PINK PLUME POPPY
Macleaya cordata
Cutting length: to 8 feet
Flower cluster length: 12 inches

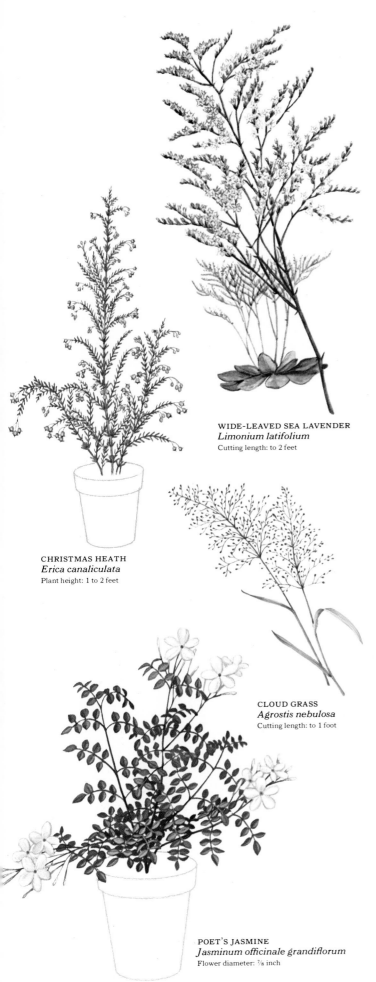

WIDE-LEAVED SEA LAVENDER
Limonium latifolium
Cutting length: to 2 feet

CHRISTMAS HEATH
Erica canaliculata
Plant height: 1 to 2 feet

CLOUD GRASS
Agrostis nebulosa
Cutting length: to 1 foot

POET'S JASMINE
Jasminum officinale grandiflorum
Flower diameter: ⅞ inch

BABIES'-BREATH. Cut babies'-breath in summer when half of the tiny flowers in a spray are open. Fresh flowers last a week if they first stand overnight in water. Recut stems under water before arranging. To dry, hang in a dark, well-ventilated place or stand in a dry vase. Babies'-breath dries in one day in silica gel. Double-flowered varieties are best for this purpose; white flowers can be dyed once dried.

CHRISTMAS HEATH. Branched stems of Christmas heath with tiny flowers and needle-like leaves are sold from fall through winter. Choose stems with half of the flowers open. Crush the stem ends and stand overnight in water. Remove leaves and flowers that will be below the water line in arrangements. Flowers hung upside down until they are dry keep their color for a year or more.

COW PARSNIP. Cut the butter-plate-sized flower heads of cow parsnip when two thirds of the florets are open. Stand overnight in water and recut the stems under water before arranging. Hang to dry.

FALSE ARALIA. The jagged-edged, finger-like, coppery- to dark-green leaves of false aralia are slender and fragile or broad and leathery, depending on their age. Give the plant bright indirect sunlight and high humidity.

FERN, FAN MAIDENHAIR. Among the laciest of house plants is the fan maidenhair fern, with its evergreen wedge-shaped leaflets that overlap along glossy, wiry black stalks. The delicate leaflets turn from pink to light green as they mature. These plants need shadowless, indirect light where night temperatures are 55° to 60°, days are 60° to 70° and humidity is about 50 per cent. To use fronds in arrangements, first submerge them in water for two hours then stand them in water until you are ready to use them.

FERN, FIJI-DAVALLIA. The hairy brown rhizomes of the Fiji-davallia fern creep over the edge of its container and can ultimately conceal a hanging basket. Delicate fronds arch gracefully. Grow this fern in shadowless indirect light. To arrange cut fronds, submerge them in cold water for two hours, then stand them in water until used. Press to dry.

GRASS, CLOUD. Pick the spikes of cloud grass in summer as the small white flowers begin to open. To use fresh, stand overnight in water. Or hang to dry.

JASMINE, POET'S. Fragrant clusters of small white flowers bloom from summer to fall amid jasmine's airy dark foliage if plants receive four hours of direct sunlight, night temperatures of 50° to 55° and day temperatures of 68° to 72°. Prune plants to control size. For arranging, cut flowers when clusters are half open and stand overnight in water; blooms will last up to a week. Dry face down in silica gel for five days.

PINK PLUME POPPY. Lacy clusters of bronze buds open to pink flowers when the plume poppy blooms in summer. For flowers that stay fresh up to four days, cut when the flower heads are half open. Split the stems, sear them with a flame and stand overnight in water. Hang to dry.

SEA LAVENDER. Wispy, delicate sprays of sea lavender last a week as cut flowers. Cut half-open flowers in the summer garden or buy them year round. Stand overnight in water. For drying, hang three-quarter-open flowers in a well-ventilated place or put in silica gel for one and one half days.

Conditioning plant materials, page 58; drying plant materials, page 67.

Rounded

Massed round shapes establish a focal point for many arrangements, their perfect balance bringing a satisfying sense of completeness to a design, whether the shapes be cut peonies or carefully placed gourds. Many decorators employ round hanging baskets, like balls suspended in space, to complement an arch or soften an angular window or corner.

GOURD
Gourd species
Fruit length: 2 inches to 5 feet

ORNAMENTAL CABBAGE
Brassica oleracea capitata
Plant diameter: 12 inches

RIEGER BEGONIA
Begonia elatior
Plant height: 1 to 1½ feet
Flower diameter: to 4 inches

CHINESE PEONY
Paeonia lactiflora
Cutting length: to 4 feet
Flower diameter: to 10 inches

GOLDEN BARREL CACTUS
Echinocactus grusonii
Plant diameter: to 3 feet

STRAWFLOWER
Helichrysum bracteatum
Cutting length: to 2 feet
Flower diameter: to 2½ inches

GLOBE THISTLE
Echinops species
Cutting length: to 4 feet
Flower head diameter: 2 to 3 inches

HARDY CHRYSANTHEMUM
Chrysanthemum morifolium
Plant height: 15 inches to 6 feet
Flower diameter: 1 to 12 inches

BEGONIA, RIEGER. Trailing varieties of tuberous-rooted begonias such as those of the Rieger hybrids are notable for their profusion of flowers up to 4 inches broad. They are often planted in hanging baskets where they can be pinched back to form 12- to 18-inch-round flower balls. In light to medium shade, tuberous-rooted begonias bloom from summer until frost. Indoors, they need bright indirect light from spring through fall, four hours of direct sunlight daily in winter. Use foliage or fully open flowers in arrangements after splitting the stems and standing them overnight in water. Then submerge each flower momentarily in cold water, turning it over to drain without shaking it. Water remaining in the petals helps keep the blossom fresh for two to four days. Spray the undersides of leaves with hair spray or plastic fixative to prevent curling. Hold the can at least 10 inches away from the leaves.

CACTUS, GOLDEN BARREL. Yellow spines line the thick ribs of this ball-shaped cactus. Yellow flowers appear if a mature plant is given bright light, 55° night and 75° or higher day temperatures during spring and summer, and 45° night and 65° day temperatures during the winter. The delicate flowers dry in silica gel in two to three days.

CHRYSANTHEMUM. Each bloom of a hardy chrysanthemum stays fresh up to three weeks, either on a potted plant or as a cut flower. Give potted chrysanthemums four hours of direct sunlight daily while they are blooming. When flowers fade, cut them back and set the plant in the garden. For arrangements, split the woody stems and stand them overnight in warm water. Then recut stems under water and remove any leaves that would be beneath the water line. Gently pinch off blemished petals.

GLOBE THISTLE. Cut the blue flower balls of globe thistles from midsummer to early fall just as they open. Split the stems and stand them overnight in water; the flowers will last about a week. Mature flowers will retain their color if they are hung to dry for about 12 days. Immature flowers dry to a soft gray-green. Spray with hair spray or plastic fixative.

GOURD. Decorative colors, patterns and textures for fall arranging are provided by gourds that range from 2-inch balls to 5-foot curved cylinders. Let the fruits ripen on the vine; harvest before the first frost when the shells are hard, leaving some stem attached. Clean them, then dry in the sun for several days. Store in a dry, cold area with good air circulation. Shine gourds with floor wax or varnish.

ORNAMENTAL CABBAGE. Cream, pink, rose or purple tinge the edges of ruffled leaves on compact heads of ornamental cabbage, most colorfully in cool weather. Leaves picked at various stages of their development and submerged overnight in water will last at least a week. Mature leaves turn a soft pink-to-purple color when laid flat to dry.

PEONY, CHINESE. Fluffy peonies last a week or more in late spring and early summer bouquets. Cut half-open flowers, split the stems and stand them overnight in water. Or dry face up in silica gel for one and one half to two days.

STRAWFLOWER. Cut brilliantly colored, half-open strawflowers as they bloom throughout the summer. To dry, arrange them in a dry vase or strip off the foliage and hang them in bunches. The dried flowers can be arranged on their own stems or given wire stems.

Conditioning plant materials, page 58; drying plant materials, page 67.

Arching

Arching plants are typically hung in windows where they give privacy or mask ugly views without blocking all of the light. Their rhythmic lines make them likely candidates for other locations too: those that do not trail beneath their containers can be placed on end tables or clustered along the floor; those that do provide proud displays on pedestals.

SAGO PALM
Cycas revoluta
Leaf length: to 2 feet

NIDULARIUM
Nidularium regelioides
Leaf cluster diameter: 18 to 24 inches

DYCKIA
Dyckia fosterana
Plant height: 1 to 2 feet

COMMON SPIDER PLANT
Chlorophytum comosum vittatum
Leaf length: 4 to 16 inches

RATTAIL CACTUS
Aporocactus flagelliformis
Stem length: to 3 feet

CHRISTMAS CACTUS
Schlumbergera-Zygocactus hybrid
Plant height: 1 to 1½ feet
Flower size: 3 inches

BURRO'S TAIL
Sedum morganianum
Stem length: to 1½ feet

BIRD'S-NEST FERN
Asplenium nidus
Plant height: 1 to 4 feet

BOSTON FERN
Nephrolepis exaltata bostoniensis
Frond length: 15 inches to 4 feet

CHINESE FAN PALM
Livistona chinensis
Leaf diameter: 1 to 5 feet

BURRO'S TAIL. Tear-shaped succulent leaves overlap on the pendant stems of burro's tail. Grow this plant where it will be undisturbed, because its leaves are easily knocked off. Provide at least four hours of direct sunlight daily.

CACTUS, RATTAIL. Inch-thick stems up to 3 feet long make the rattail cactus a conversation piece as a hanging-basket plant. This fountain of stems, densely covered with yellow-brown spines, bears small pink flowers in late spring. Provide at least four hours of direct sunlight daily.

CHRISTMAS CACTUS. Pendant flowers in brilliant colors tip the flattened stems of Christmas cacti in winter. Provide bright indirect sunlight during spring and summer and temperatures of 60° at night and 70° or higher by day once buds set. But water sparingly, withhold fertilizer and keep the plant at a temperature of 55° in November and December, the resting period, to encourage flowering.

DYCKIA. The stiff, arching, succulent leaves of dyckias are green or gray on top and edged with spines. Slender 1- to 2-foot spikes clustered with waxy yellow, orange or red flowers grow from the rosettes' centers in summer. Like other bromeliads, dyckias require direct or lightly filtered sunlight.

FERN, BIRD'S-NEST. The gently arching, broad, leathery fronds of this fern form a bird's-nest shape and grow out of a hairy, fibrous crown covered with hairy, dark scales. Used as an accent plant, this fern requires only low levels of indirect light but it needs humidity of 50 per cent or more and 50° to 60° night temperatures.

FERN, BOSTON. Since Victorian times the Boston fern has been valued for its pendant fronds crowded with rich green leaflets. When grown on a pedestal or in a hanging basket, it gracefully cascades downward, often hiding its container. Provide curtain-filtered sunlight and humidity of 50 per cent or more and avoid touching the fronds. Cut fronds can be used in arrangements after being submerged lengthwise in cold water for four hours.

NIDULARIUM. Broad, flat rosettes of arching leaves form cups for nidularium's inconspicuous flowers. Before the blossoms appear, the center of the rosette becomes brightly colored, usually red. The light green leaves may have spiny edges and be striped, spotted or blotched, depending on the species. Give these bromeliads bright indirect sunlight and keep water in the cup formed by the leaves.

PALM, CHINESE FAN. Umbrellas of arching, semicircular leaves resembling open paper fans make the Chinese fan palm a graceful specimen plant. The fans grow larger as plants mature. Provide bright indirect sunlight. Leaves can be used in fresh arrangements or preserved with glycerin.

PALM, SAGO. Like a clump of green-toothed combs, the sago palm's leathery leaves arch and spread from a stubby trunk. Place a sago palm where its fronds will not be touched and use no pesticide on it.

SPIDER PLANT. Grown either in a flowerpot or in a hanging container, the spider plant produces small plantlets on cascading stems that grow among the grasslike leaves. You can remove and root these new plants or, if space allows a grand cascade, leave them on hanging plants until they form plantlets of their own.

Conditioning plant materials, page 58; preserving in glycerin, page 70.

Spiky

Spiky shapes make a flower arrangement seem tall, whether used in a mass of flowers in the Western tradition or as the crowning point of a spare Oriental composition. Because a vertical shape leads the eye upward, designers use spiky plants to complement similar shapes, such as tall windows, or to draw attention higher, as to a group of hanging baskets.

COMMON FOXGLOVE
Digitalis purpurea
Cutting length: to 5 feet

CAROLINA THERMOPSIS
Thermopsis caroliniana
Cutting length: to 4 feet
Flower spike height: 10 to 12 inches

MINIATURE GLADIOLUS
Gladiolus species and hybrids
Cutting length: 1 to 5 feet

TRUE LAVENDER
Lavandula officinalis
Cutting length: 1 to 3 feet

RUBY GRASS
Rhynchelytrum repens
Cutting length: to 4 feet

SANSEVIERIA
Sansevieria trifasciata
Plant height: 4 to 30 inches

SNAPDRAGON
Antirrhinum majus
Cutting length: 6 inches to 4 feet

OXTONGUE GASTERIA
Gasteria verrucosa
Leaf length: 6 inches

FOXGLOVE. Spikes of foxglove in the summer garden provide cut flowers that will last five to 10 days. Cut half-open spikes and stand them overnight in warm water. Remove lower florets as they fade; recondition wilting spikes by recutting stems and placing in warm water. Dry foxgloves for three to four days in silica gel by placing spikes lengthwise and filling the flower bells. Protect dried blossoms with hair spray or plastic fixative.

GASTERIA, OXTONGUE. The fleshy pointed leaves of this easy-to-grow succulent are marked with tiny white spots. The clump of leaves grows 6 inches tall, a good size for use on a table. Grow in bright indirect light.

GLADIOLUS. Cut spikes of gladiolus from late summer to early fall or buy them year round. Choose spikes that have only one open blossom. Flowers last longer if tissues are soft initially; cut in midafternoon or keep cut blooms out of water for 30 minutes. Recut and split stems before standing them overnight in water. If these stems stand at an angle, tips of the spikes will turn up. Individual flowers last two days and should be removed as they fade. A spike lasts one to two weeks in a fresh arrangement. Both flowers and foliage can be dried. Dry flowers and stems separately after hooking wire through each flower head. Flowers dry face up in one and one half days in silica gel; they are fragile and wilt in high humidity unless coated with hair spray. Treat foliage with glycerin or stand it in a jar to dry.

GRASS, RUBY. Spiky plumes of ruby grass gradually turn from wine red to purple as they age. Cut when the plumes are half open. To get graceful, curved stems, stand them upright in a vase without water and allow them to dry. For straight stems, hang upside down to dry.

LAVENDER, TRUE. For fragrant leaves and flowers, cut spikes of lavender in the summer when half the flowers are open. Split the ends of the stems and stand them overnight in water. Flowers last a week in arrangements. Hang flower spikes and foliage to dry, or place them in silica gel for one and one half days.

SANSEVIERIA. An almost indestructible house plant, sansevieria survives in dim light and thrives in bright indirect light. The stiff, narrow leaves can be cut for use in fresh or dried arrangements. Wash the leaves, then rub with olive oil to make them shine. Leaves will dry in the arrangement. They also can be dried flat on a newspaper.

SNAPDRAGON. Cut snapdragon spikes in summer when half the florets are open and stand them overnight in water that contains a commercial floral preservative. Recut and recondition purchased flowers. As individual florets wilt, snip them off. Spikes last five to 12 days in floral arrangements. To dry snapdragons, place them lengthwise in silica gel for three to four days.

THERMOPSIS. Covered with pealike blossoms, spikes of thermopsis appear in the summer garden about the same time as delphiniums, so these two kinds of flowers are frequently combined in fresh arrangements. Cut when half the flowers are open, split the ends of the stems and stand them in cold water overnight (warm water causes deterioration). Place some stems at a slant so that they will produce curves. Spikes last a week or more. Hang to dry or place in silica gel for three to four days.

Conditioning plant materials, page 58; drying plant materials, page 67; preserving in glycerin, page 70.

Sculptural

Plants with dramatically drooping, twisting or angular silhouettes have long been favored by interior designers, who employ their sculptural shapes to provide a focal point for a room, to draw the eye from an architectural oddity or simply to serve as objets d'art, holding their own in competition with almost any man-made creation.

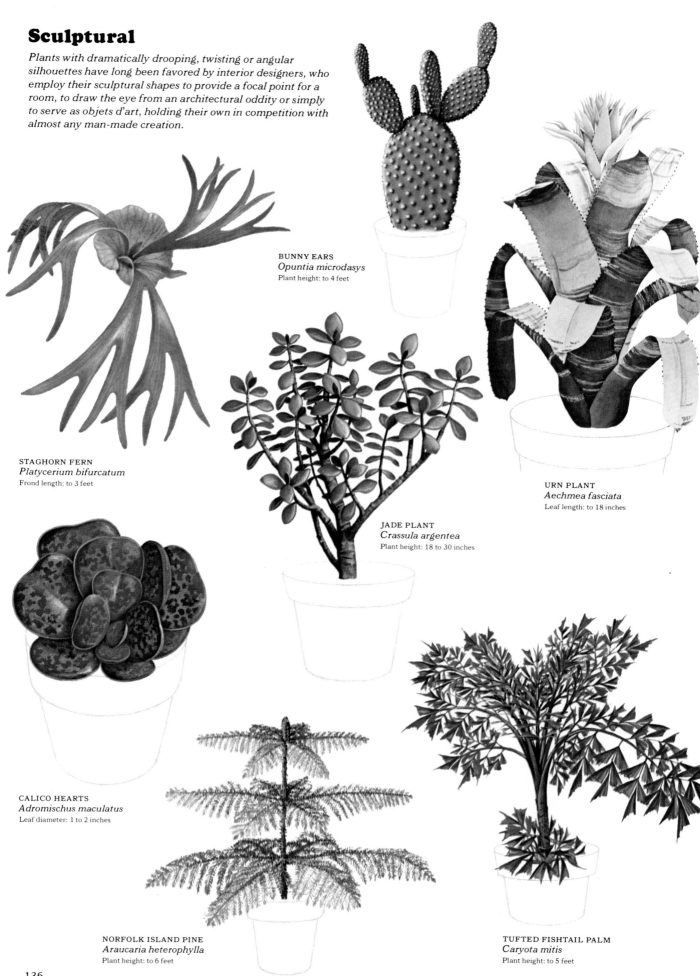

BUNNY EARS
Opuntia microdasys
Plant height: to 4 feet

STAGHORN FERN
Platycerium bifurcatum
Frond length: to 3 feet

JADE PLANT
Crassula argentea
Plant height: 18 to 30 inches

URN PLANT
Aechmea fasciata
Leaf length: to 18 inches

CALICO HEARTS
Adromischus maculatus
Leaf diameter: 1 to 2 inches

NORFOLK ISLAND PINE
Araucaria heterophylla
Plant height: to 6 feet

TUFTED FISHTAIL PALM
Caryota mitis
Plant height: to 5 feet

136

QUEEN VICTORIA CENTURY PLANT
Agave victoriae-reginae
Leaf length: 4 to 6 inches

ELEPHANT-FOOT TREE
Beaucarnea recurvata
Plant height: to 30 feet

MILK-STRIPED EUPHORBIA
Euphorbia lactea
Plant height: 3 feet

CACTUS, BUNNY-EARS. Named for the branching growth of its paddle-shaped green stems, the bunny-ears cactus is a living sculpture to look at but not touch. The flat pads are dotted with clusters of white, yellow or red-brown prickly growths that are extremely irritating to the skin. Provide at least four hours of direct sunlight daily.

CALICO HEARTS. The plump, stemless, gray-green leaves of calico hearts, spotted reddish brown, form novel eye-catching clumps in dish gardens or pots. Provide at least four hours of direct sunlight daily.

CENTURY PLANT. An extremely slow-growing succulent, the century plant forms a compact mound of stiff, sword-shaped leaves that frequently have needle-like points at their tips and sharp teeth along their edges. The Queen Victoria century plant is a small species with leaves that are edged and marked with white. A century plant grows best with four hours of direct sunlight daily.

ELEPHANT-FOOT TREE. The grayish-brown, wrinkled trunk of the elephant-foot tree is greatly swollen at its base. A fountain of grasslike leaves, up to 4 feet long, cascades from the top. Provide four hours of direct sunlight daily.

FERN, STAGHORN. Branched like antlers, leathery gray or green staghorn-fern fronds dangle like abstract mobiles. Closely packed spore masses appear on the undersides of the frond tips, covering them with soft brown fuzz when mature. Hang them where they will receive bright indirect sunlight, with humidity of 50 per cent or more.

JADE PLANT. Shiny oval leaves clustered along fleshy, branching stems give a mature jade plant the look of a miniature tree. Group young plants in dish gardens, then display them singly as accent plants once they branch and develop trunks. This succulent tolerates temperatures as low as 40° and requires four hours of direct light daily.

MILK-STRIPED EUPHORBIA. Sometimes called the candelabra cactus, the milk-striped euphorbia's triangular stem and branches are streaked with white and edged with stout thorns. This vertical plant slowly grows to a height of 3 feet or more. Provide four hours of direct sunlight daily.

NORFOLK ISLAND PINE. Noted for its symmetry, the pyramid-shaped Norfolk Island pine has tiers of horizontal branches with gracefully drooping tips spaced at regular intervals along its woody trunk. These tropical evergreens, with soft, glossy needles, grow slowly to 6 feet or more indoors. Give Norfolk Island pines bright indirect light most of the year, some direct sunlight in winter. Temperatures ranging from 50° at night to 72° by day are best.

PALM, TUFTED FISHTAIL. A canopy of wedge-shaped leathery leaflets makes the tufted fishtail palm outstanding as a floor plant. The cluster of smooth stems, each topped by an arching frond, grows 6 to 8 inches a year to a height of 5 feet. Provide bright indirect light.

URN PLANT. Growing in a tight rosette, the urn plant's broad, leathery leaves form a water-holding cup at the center. The stiffly arching foliage is banded with silver. Display the plant so its symmetry can be appreciated from above. Provide four hours of bright indirect sunlight daily and keep the cup filled with water.

TEXTURES: Rough

Rough-textured, light-absorbing plant materials are particularly at home in a casual, informal setting, where they can be used in the same way as nubbly fabric or textured paneling. They also work well as accents in a modern decorating scheme where they stand out boldly amid smooth chrome and plastic. Their tactile quality adds dimension to flower arrangements.

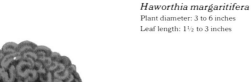

BUTTERNUT
Juglans cinerea
Nut kernel length: 1½ to 2 inches

PEARLY HAWORTHIA
Haworthia margaritifera
Plant diameter: 3 to 6 inches
Leaf length: 1½ to 3 inches

OLD-MAN CACTUS
Cephalocereus senilis
Plant height: to 1 foot

COCKSCOMB
Celosia argentea cristata
Cutting length: 6 inches to 3 feet
Flower head diameter: 2 to 10 inches

CHINESE CHESTNUT
Castanea mollissima
Seed husk diameter: 2 to 3 inches

PANAMIGA
Pilea involucrata
Plant height: 6 to 8 inches

GOLDEN EASTER LILY CACTUS
Lobivia aurea
Plant height: 4 inches

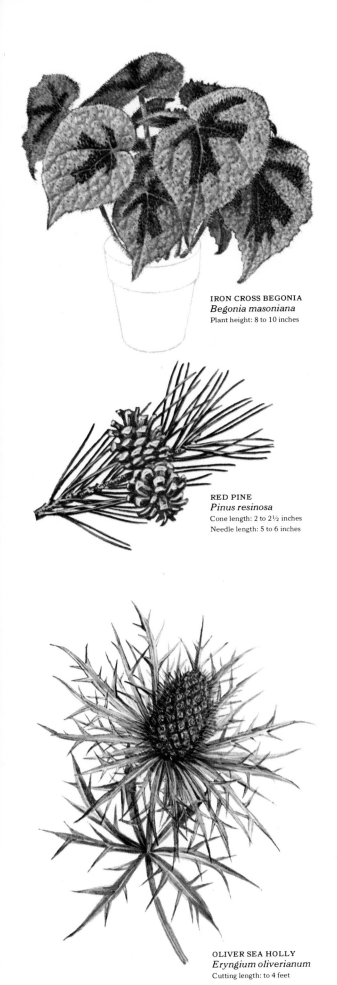

IRON CROSS BEGONIA
Begonia masoniana
Plant height: 8 to 10 inches

RED PINE
Pinus resinosa
Cone length: 2 to 2½ inches
Needle length: 5 to 6 inches

OLIVER SEA HOLLY
Eryngium oliverianum
Cutting length: to 4 feet

BEGONIA, IRON CROSS. Fanciful common names like iron cross, beefsteak and stitchleaf suggest the patterned, frequently hairy or bumpy surfaces of leaves growing along the succulent creeping stems of rhizomatous begonias. Keep them in bright indirect sunlight from spring through fall and provide some direct sunlight in winter. Cut leaves last four to seven days in arrangements if stems are first split and left standing in water overnight. Spray the undersides of cut leaves with hair spray to keep them from curling.

BUTTERNUT. Use deeply ridged butternuts in arrangements after drying them in shallow layers. Nuts may be spray-painted, waxed or bleached to achieve various effects.

CACTUS, GOLDEN EASTER LILY. A cylindrical dwarf resembling a corncob, the Easter lily cactus has notched ribs lined with flat yellow spines. For flowers up to 4 inches across in early summer, keep it cool in winter—40° to 45° at night and under 65° during the day. During the rest of the year, it needs about 70° at night and 85° during the day.

CACTUS, OLD-MAN. If you squint as you view the ridged, foot-high column of an old-man cactus, covered with long, drooping white hairs and shorter yellow spines, it is easy to imagine a grizzled desert hermit. The plant grows best in direct sunlight. Provide it with night temperatures of 40° to 45° in winter, 65° to 70° in other seasons, and day temperatures about 10° higher.

CHESTNUT, CHINESE. Wear gloves when you gather prickly chestnuts in late summer. Swish them in soapy water, let drain and remove the husks.

COCKSCOMB. Bearing brilliant red, yellow, orange or purple flowers, cockscombs bloom from summer through frost. Depending on the species, the flower heads look like velvety fans, feathery plumes or woolly balls. Cut them when the flowers reach the desired size but before seeds set. Stand them overnight in water. Flowers last one to three weeks. To dry, strip off the foliage and hang, or preserve with glycerin. Dried cockscombs fade in strong light.

HAWORTHIA, PEARLY. Thick, wedge-shaped haworthia leaves are banded across their backs with white wartlike growths. The pointed upturned leaves grow in small compact clusters. Place them in bright indirect sunlight.

PANAMIGA. The copper, bronze, green or silver leaves of most panamigas look as if they are quilted. Give these plants bright indirect light and temperatures ranging from 65° at night up to 85° by day.

PINE, RED. Long flexible branches cut from pine trees last several weeks indoors. Wash in warm, soapy water, then stand them overnight in water with one tablespoon of glycerin added per quart. Air-dried pine remains green for several months, but branches may also be preserved by treating them with glycerin for ten days. Collect cones in late autumn and scrub them in warm, soapy water, then dry in a 250° oven. To keep cones closed, coat them with plastic spray.

SEA HOLLY. Cut spiny sea-holly flowers in summer when they are fully opened. The flowers will last several weeks if first kept standing overnight in water. Or dry by removing leaves and hanging flowers in a dark, well-ventilated place. Dried flowers retain their blue color.

Conditioning plant materials, page 58; drying plant materials, page 67; wiring nuts and cones, page 69; preserving in glycerin, page 70.

Feathery

Feathery plants, with their light, almost intangible textures, are used in arrangements as a soft backdrop. In a decorating scheme, a group of finely textured plants seems to enlarge space by creating an illusion of distance. Their indefinite edges complement lush materials such as velvet, fur and suede. Placed in a window, they cast elegant and complex shadows.

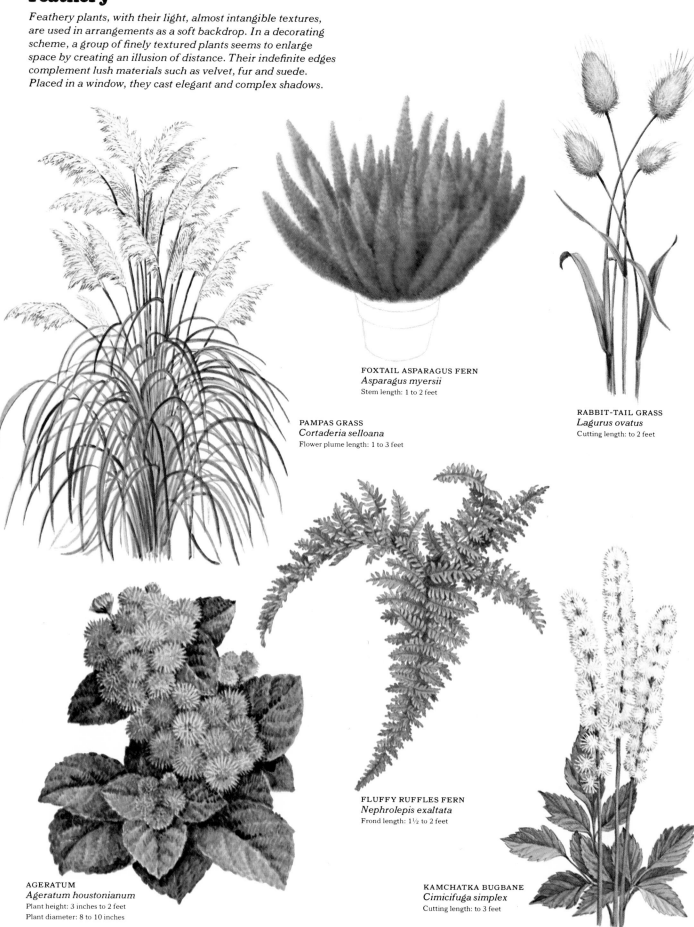

FOXTAIL ASPARAGUS FERN
Asparagus myersii
Stem length: 1 to 2 feet

PAMPAS GRASS
Cortaderia selloana
Flower plume length: 1 to 3 feet

RABBIT-TAIL GRASS
Lagurus ovatus
Cutting length: to 2 feet

FLUFFY RUFFLES FERN
Nephrolepis exaltata
Frond length: 1½ to 2 feet

AGERATUM
Ageratum houstonianum
Plant height: 3 inches to 2 feet
Plant diameter: 8 to 10 inches

KAMCHATKA BUGBANE
Cimicifuga simplex
Cutting length: to 3 feet

MIGNONETTE
Reseda odorata
Cutting length: to 1½ feet

CHINESE PODOCARPUS
Podocarpus macrophyllus maki
Plant height: 6 feet

SQUIRRELTAIL GRASS
Hordeum jubatum
Cutting length: 9 inches to 3 feet

ASTILBE
Astilbe arendsii
Cutting length: to 3 feet
Flower plume length: 8 to 12 inches

AGERATUM. Grown in direct sunlight, ageratum forms compact mounds covered with tiny, fuzzy flowers. Choose low varieties for window boxes and hanging baskets. Use taller varieties for cut flowers, picking them when half of the flowers are open. Cut flowers will last one week if first left standing overnight in warm water. Flowers can be dried hanging or standing in a dry vase, but those dried in silica gel for one and one half to two days retain the best color.

ASPARAGUS FERN. Wiry, arching branches crowded with tiny, flat green stems give ornamental asparagus species the filmy, billowy look associated with ferns, although they are botanically unrelated. Give them bright indirect light. Cuttings of asparagus fern can be held in the refrigerator in plastic bags without water for up to two weeks. For immediate use, stand branches overnight in water.

ASTILBE. Plumes of tiny flowers on stalks up to 3 feet tall bloom amid the astilbe's mound of fernlike deep-green or bronze foliage. Cut when the flower clusters are half open, split the stems and stand overnight in water. Flowers last one week. Dried flowers and seed heads retain their color well. Hang fully open flowers upside down or place horizontally in silica gel for one and one half days.

BUGBANE. In late summer and fall, bugbane bears tiny white flowers on 2-foot spires that are excellent for cutting. Stand stems overnight in water and recut under water before arranging. Flowers last five to seven days. To dry, hang or place horizontally in silica gel for one and one half days.

FERN, FLUFFY RUFFLES. The crisp fronds of the Fluffy Ruffles fern, a variant of the popular Boston fern, are tightly packed with frilled and curly leaflets. They grow in a low level of indirect light but need humidity of 50 to 60 per cent. For arrangements, submerge fronds in cold water for four hours, then stand stems in cold water until needed.

GRASS, PAMPAS. Growing to 10 feet or more, pampas grass stalks can be dried for vertical accents where light is inadequate for living plants. Cut the silky, silvery-white-to-pink flowers in fall and hang or stand in a container to dry.

GRASS, RABBIT-TAIL. Dense, woolly seed puffs up to 2 inches long make rabbit-tail grass a fluffy accent plant. Use in fresh arrangements after conditioning overnight in water. Hang in a dark place to dry.

GRASS, SQUIRRELTAIL. The pastel-colored flowers that bloom in the summer turn to beige as squirreltail grass ages and dries in the garden. Gather at various stages of maturity for a variety of colors. To use in fresh arrangements, condition stems in cold water overnight. Hang to dry, or treat with glycerin for more flexible stems.

MIGNONETTE. The noteworthy fragrance of mignonette more than compensates for its undistinguished flowers. Cut when half open, flowers last five to seven days in arrangements after standing overnight in water.

PODOCARPUS, CHINESE. An indoor evergreen that can grow 6 feet tall, podocarpus may be pruned as desired. Its soft-textured needles age from bright to dark green. Give it four hours of direct sunlight daily or longer periods of very bright indirect light. Cut branches last one to three weeks if stems are split and left standing overnight in water.

Conditioning plant materials, page 58; drying plant materials, page 67; preserving in glycerin, page 70.

Waxy

Seemingly as smooth as silk with a gleam like that of polished mahogany, plant materials with waxy surfaces possess a reflecting quality that brings highlights into any arrangement. Designers employ this smooth texture either to maintain continuity in a sleek, modern interior or to add a note of contrast in a roughhewn, casual one.

COMMON CAMELLIA
Camellia japonica
Flower diameter: 2 to 5 inches

BROAD-LEAVED INDIA-RUBBER TREE
Ficus elastica decora
Plant height: 5 to 8 feet

JAPANESE PITTOSPORUM
Pittosporum tobira
Plant height: 3 to 6 feet

APPLE
Malus varieties
Fruit diameter: 2 to 4 inches

MOONSTONES
Pachyphytum oviferum
Plant height: 6 inches

PEPPER PLANT
Capsicum annuum conoides
Plant height: to 1 foot

SOUTHERN MAGNOLIA
Magnolia grandiflora
Leaf length: 6 to 10 inches
Flower diameter: 8 to 14 inches

WAX PLANT
Hoya carnosa
Stem length: 2 to 3 feet
Flower cluster diameter: 3 to 4 inches

APPLE. Use apples decoratively after rubbing their skins to a high shine or coating them with clear lacquer.

CAMELLIA. Glossy-leaved indoor camellias bloom between late fall and early spring if temperatures are 60° to 65° at night in summer when buds are set and from 40° to 45° at night while they are in flower. Cut partly open blossoms with a few leaves, split the stem ends and stand overnight in water. Mist daily to prolong freshness. Flowers last three to eight days in arrangements. Camellias can be dried in two to four days face up in silica gel. Preserve leaves with glycerin.

MAGNOLIA, SOUTHERN. Appearing throughout spring and summer among glossy, dark green leaves, the waxy flowers of southern magnolias last only a day or two in arrangements. Cut well-developed buds in late afternoon for fully opened flowers the next day. Split the woody branches, scrape the bark away at the base, and stand overnight in water. If necessary, gently force petals open in cold water. Submerge open flowers in cold water until petals are crisp and firm. Pick branches with leaf buds in spring or fall and hang them upside down to dry. In fall, collect brown seed pods with red seeds inside and hang to dry. Magnolia leaves keep indefinitely when treated with glycerin.

MOONSTONES. The fat, plump succulent leaves of moonstones are eye-catchers. The green leaves take on a pink hue if the plants receive at least four hours of direct sun daily.

PEPPER PLANT. The shiny, conical fruits that rise above the ornamental pepper's glossy green foliage ripen gradually to yellow, red or purple. Grow them outdoors or indoors where they receive at least four hours of direct sunlight daily. Hung upside down to dry, the fruits remain colorful.

PITTOSPORUM, JAPANESE. The shiny, oval evergreen leaves of Japanese pittosporum resemble rhododendron foliage. The small creamy flowers have an orange-blossom fragrance. Give plants four or more hours of direct sunlight and prune to shape them. Use cuttings in arrangements.

PRIVET, WAX-LEAVED. The glossy wax-leaved privet grows well indoors if it receives at least four hours of direct sunlight daily. It can reach 6 feet but may be pruned. Cut older foliage of outdoor privets year round. Cut flowering branches when clusters are half open, split stems and stand overnight in cold water. When branches are hung to dry, flowers turn pale cream, but fruits retain their color. Treated with glycerin, foliage turns golden brown.

RUBBER TREE. Large, smooth, waxy leaves have made the rubber tree a favorite decorative house plant. The thick, raised rib running the length of each dark green leaf is often colorful and the leaves of some varieties are mottled. Young rubber trees are suitable for table display but they soon must be moved to floor containers. Rubber trees can be maintained in dim light but grow best in bright indirect light.

WAX PLANT. The twining vines of some wax plant varieties have thick leaves sometimes marked with creamy white and pink. Clusters of waxy, fragrant, white or pink star-shaped flowers usually bloom during summer and fall. Train plants to trellises and place them where they will receive four hours of direct sun or very bright indirect light. Keep the soil moist while plants are in flower, but let it dry almost completely between waterings during winter dormancy.

WAX-LEAVED PRIVET
Ligustrum japonicum
Plant height: to 6 feet

Conditioning plant materials, page 58; drying plant materials, page 67; preserving in glycerin, page 70.

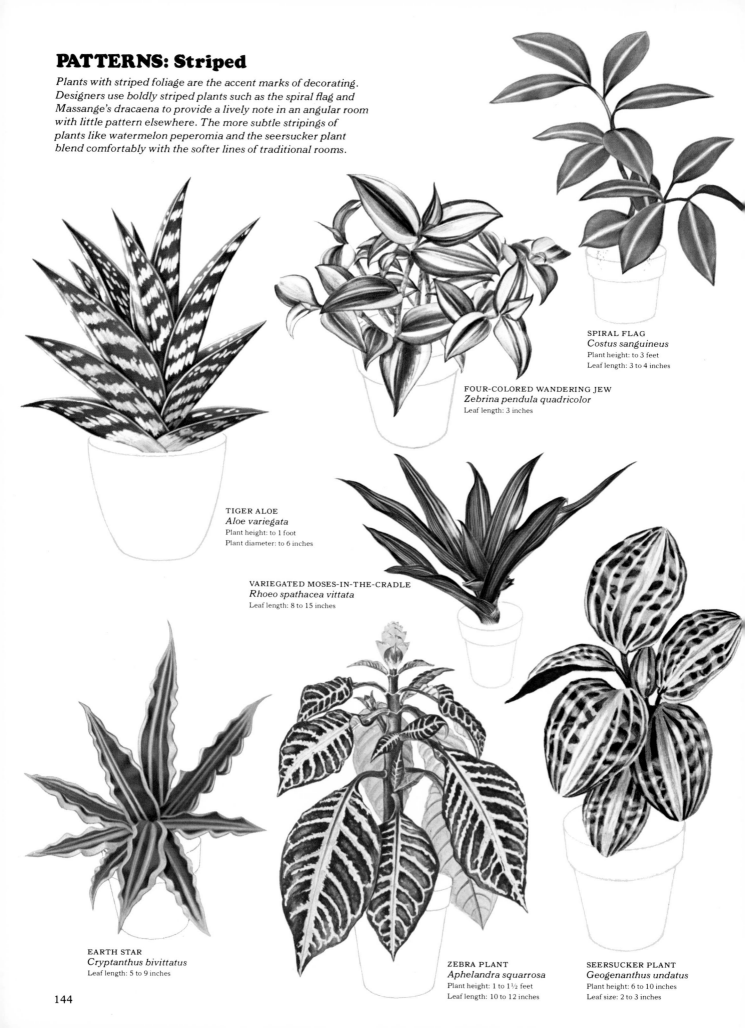

PATTERNS: Striped

Plants with striped foliage are the accent marks of decorating.
Designers use boldly striped plants such as the spiral flag and
Massange's dracaena to provide a lively note in an angular room
with little pattern elsewhere. The more subtle stripings of
plants like watermelon peperomia and the seersucker plant
blend comfortably with the softer lines of traditional rooms.

SPIRAL FLAG
Costus sanguineus
Plant height: to 3 feet
Leaf length: 3 to 4 inches

FOUR-COLORED WANDERING JEW
Zebrina pendula quadricolor
Leaf length: 3 inches

TIGER ALOE
Aloe variegata
Plant height: to 1 foot
Plant diameter: to 6 inches

VARIEGATED MOSES-IN-THE-CRADLE
Rhoeo spathacea vittata
Leaf length: 8 to 15 inches

EARTH STAR
Cryptanthus bivittatus
Leaf length: 5 to 9 inches

ZEBRA PLANT
Aphelandra squarrosa
Plant height: 1 to 1½ feet
Leaf length: 10 to 12 inches

SEERSUCKER PLANT
Geogenanthus undatus
Plant height: 6 to 10 inches
Leaf size: 2 to 3 inches

MASSANGE'S DRACAENA
Dracaena fragrans massangeana
Plant height: to 6 feet
Leaf length: 18 to 30 inches

WATERMELON PEPEROMIA
Peperomia sandersii
Plant height: 8 to 10 inches
Leaf size: 2 to 4 inches

STRIPED INCH PLANT
Callisia elegans
Leaf size: 1 to 1½ inches

ALOE, TIGER. Ideal for a sunny window sill, the succulent aloe is prized for its rosette of thick, triangular leaves. Foliage of various species grows from 4 to 20 inches long and is sometimes striped with color. Tiger aloe's leaves are irregularly banded with white. At least four hours of direct sunlight daily assures compact growth and clear markings.

DRACAENA, MASSANGE'S. Straplike leaves that telescope from one another to form sturdy green stems give young specimens of Massange's dracaena another common name, corn plant. The arching foliage is striped with yellow. Decorative in a window garden or on a coffee table when young, this dracaena eventually develops a 6-foot stem with a tuft of foliage on top and is particularly useful in a floor container. Place the plant where it will receive bright indirect sunlight. Dracaena leaves last up to two weeks in arrangements. Cut the leaf as close to its base as possible. Split the base of the leaf and stand it overnight in water.

EARTH STAR. The leathery leaves of the earth star, which form a flat rosette up to 1½ feet across, are striped with brilliant patterns. Depending on the species, the olive- or bronze-green leaves are striped with such colors as red, purple or cream, and the leaf edges are often wavy, spiny or both. Strong indirect sunlight is essential to prevent fading.

MOSES-IN-THE-CRADLE. Tiny white flowers cradled between thin petal-like bracts among the foliage give Moses-in-the-cradle its name. The sword-shaped leaves are striped with purple, green and sometimes yellow. It grows best in bright indirect sunlight.

PEPEROMIA, WATERMELON. The pattern of green and silver stripes on the glossy leaves of a watermelon peperomia resembles the rind of the plant's namesake fruit. Give peperomias bright indirect light. Leaves root in water and can be used in arrangements.

SEERSUCKER PLANT. Puckered leaves striped with metallic green and gray give this plant the look and texture of a seersucker fabric. Place it on a window sill where it will get bright indirect sunlight.

SPIRAL FLAG. Unusual in both color and habit of growth, spiral flag has blue-green leaves marked with silver stripes; they grow in a spiral around red stems. Give the plant curtain-filtered sunlight.

STRIPED INCH PLANT. In a hanging basket, the striped inch plant cascades freely so both sides of its fleshy leaves, striped with white above and solid purple on the underside, can be seen. For best color, the plant needs bright indirect light. Pinch it back often to promote branching.

WANDERING JEW. Leaves irregularly striped with pink, purple, red, green and white make many wandering Jews a source of color throughout the year. Easy to cultivate, the trailing stems look best in a hanging basket where they can display their color. Provide bright indirect light and pinch back frequently to assure bushiness.

ZEBRA PLANT. Pointed oval leaves marked with ivory along their veins make the zebra plant a dramatic accent on a table or in a low plant grouping. Spikes of gaudy yellow flowers appear above the leaves for about six weeks, usually in fall. Provide bright indirect light and high humidity.

Conditioning plant materials, page 58.

Spotted

On flowers and plants, as on fabrics, spots dance and create visual excitement. Splashy spots like those of monkey flowers fairly spin while the more delicate markings of kohleria produce a quieter rhythm. Spotted plants and flowers sound a gay note in informal settings. They also enliven sedate rooms and flower arrangements that would seem dull without them.

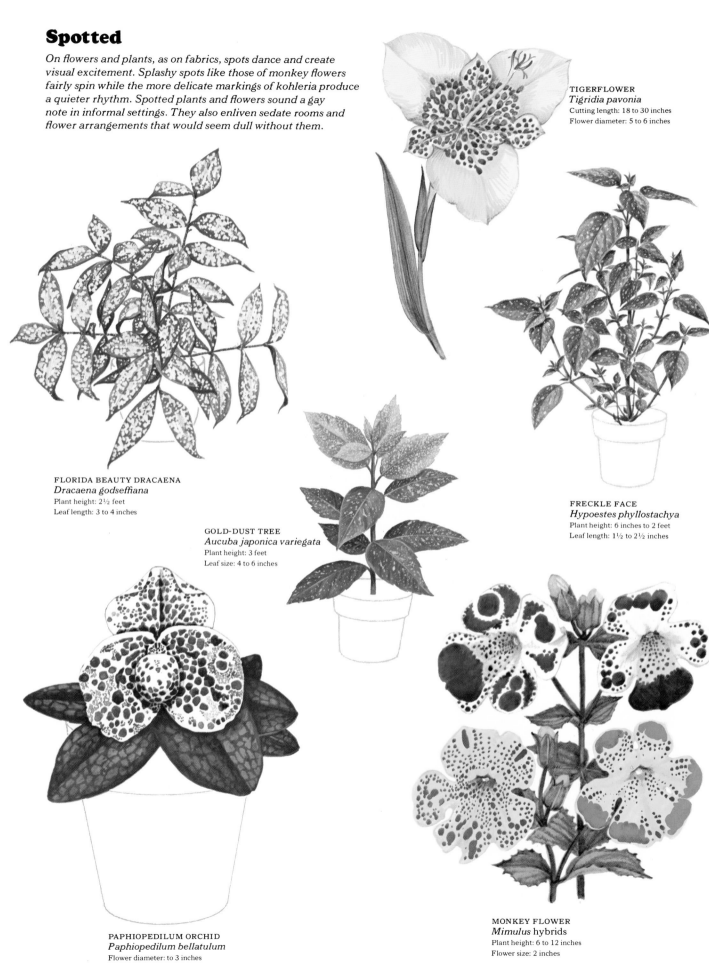

TIGERFLOWER
Tigridia pavonia
Cutting length: 18 to 30 inches
Flower diameter: 5 to 6 inches

FLORIDA BEAUTY DRACAENA
Dracaena godseffiana
Plant height: 2½ feet
Leaf length: 3 to 4 inches

GOLD-DUST TREE
Aucuba japonica variegata
Plant height: 3 feet
Leaf size: 4 to 6 inches

FRECKLE FACE
Hypoestes phyllostachya
Plant height: 6 inches to 2 feet
Leaf length: 1½ to 2½ inches

PAPHIOPEDILUM ORCHID
Paphiopedilum bellatulum
Flower diameter: to 3 inches

MONKEY FLOWER
Mimulus hybrids
Plant height: 6 to 12 inches
Flower size: 2 inches

146

POCKETBOOK FLOWER
Calceolaria herbeohybrida
Plant height: 6 to 12 inches
Flower diameter: to 2 inches

ORIENTAL HYBRID LILY
Lilium species and hybrids
Cutting length: 1 to 8 feet
Flower diameter: 2 to 12 inches

KOHLERIA
Kohleria amabilis
Plant height: 8 to 30 inches
Flower size: 2 inches

DRACAENA FLORIDA BEAUTY. The pointed oval leaves of Florida Beauty dracaena are so heavily splashed with yellow and white that little of the basic green shows. For best growth and color, provide bright indirect light. Cut foliage lasts two weeks. Sever branches just above the point where leaves begin, wash, split stem ends, and stand overnight in water. Glycerin-treated foliage lasts indefinitely.

FRECKLE FACE. Irregular pink speckles add pastel interest to the hairy leaves that grow densely along the freckle-face plant's branching stems. Provide bright indirect light.

GOLD-DUST TREE. A house plant able to withstand both cold and drafts, the gold-dust tree has shiny green leaves flecked with yellow. Place it where it will receive bright indirect light. Branches last for weeks in arrangements and eventually root in water. Split the stem ends and stand them overnight in water.

KOHLERIA. Contrasting colors spot the tubular flowers that grow among kohleria's thick, hairy leaves. Most varieties are at their best when used as hanging plants, but a few grow upright. Provide bright indirect light.

LILY. Large, fragrant flower trumpets streaked and dotted with contrasting hues bloom from early summer through fall on tall garden lilies. When cutting, select stems with at least two open flowers. Split the stem ends before placing in deep water overnight; recut under water before arranging. Pinch off the orange pollen-bearing anthers to prevent stains on tablecloths or clothing. Flowers last up to two weeks. Or wire flower heads and dry in silica gel for two to four days. The brown seed pods are also used in arrangements.

MONKEY FLOWER. Boldly splashed and dotted monkey flowers are shade- and moisture-loving annuals that can be grown indoors in bright indirect sunlight. Cut when fully open and stand overnight in water; they will last five days.

ORCHID, PAPHIOPEDILUM. Many varieties of this tropical orchid have both mottled leaves and flowers. Blossoms last up to three months on plants grown in filtered sunlight. Choose fully open flowers for cutting. Place stems in water vials or tape moistened pieces of cotton to the cut ends and refrigerate until used. Check the water level daily. Place corsages in the refrigerator when they are not being worn, and keep orchid arrangements in cool rooms.

POCKETBOOK FLOWER. Unusual in both its shape and its coloring, the inflated pouchlike lower lips of pocketbook flowers are heavily spotted with contrasting colors. Purchase blooming plants in the spring and keep them in bright indirect light where temperatures range from 40° at night up to 60° by day. Discard plants after they flower. For fresh flowers lasting three to five days, cut when half of a flower cluster is open, split the stem end and stand it overnight in water, taking care not to wet the petals.

TIGERFLOWER. Two triangular tiers of petals, a larger outer layer usually of a single hue and a heavily spotted inner ring, comprise the big blossom of the summer-blooming tigerflower. Although individual flowers last only a day, each stem produces up to six flowers over a six- to eight-week period. Cut when one or two blossoms are fully open, stand stems one to two hours in water, then recut the stems under water before arranging.

Conditioning plant materials, page 58; preserving in glycerin, page 70; drying plant materials, page 67.

Variegated

Variegated plants and flowers make light of every rule about combining shapes and colors. Their eclectic mix of patterns, textures and colors is often startling. Position them as focal points in low-key decorating schemes, let them echo patterns in Oriental rugs or fabrics, or group several types to make a living patchwork quilt.

PANSY
Viola species
Cutting length: 6 to 12 inches
Flower diameter: ¾ to 4 inches

COLEUS
Coleus blumei
Plant height: 6 inches to 2 feet
Leaf length: 1 to 4 inches

CROTON
Codiaeum variegatum
Plant height: 3 to 5 feet

PRAYER PLANT
Maranta leuconeura
Plant height: 6 to 8 inches
Leaf length: to 6 inches

WHITE-EDGED SWEDISH IVY
Plectranthus coleoides marginatus
Plant height: 8 to 12 inches
Leaf size: 2 to 3 inches

BEGONIA TREEBINE
Cissus discolor
Leaf size: 3 to 4 inches

SILVER-NERVED FITTONIA
Fittonia argyoneura
Leaf size: 2 to 4 inches

EMERALD 'N GOLD WINTER CREEPER
Euonymus fortunei
Leaf length: 1 to 2 inches

VANDA ORCHID
Vanda rothschildiana
Flower diameter: 3 to 6 inches

PAINTED TONGUE
Salpiglossis sinuata
Plant height: 1½ to 3 feet
Flower diameter: 2 to 2½ inches

BEGONIA TREEBINE. Quilted leaves that are striped and splotched with green, silver and purple make the begonia treebine one of the most colorful foliage plants. It is a climbing plant that can be trained to a stake or trellis, and it also will trail from a basket. Place it in bright indirect light.

COLEUS. Brilliantly colored leaves in paisley-like patterns are a coleus hallmark. Grow these plants in sunlight or partial shade, indoors on a bright window sill where they get at least four hours of direct sun daily. Pinch back often to spur bushy growth. Use the vivid leaves in arrangements after splitting stem ends and standing them overnight in water. Cuttings often root in water in two to three weeks.

CROTON. Vibrant shades of green, yellow, orange, pink, red, copper, brown and ivory may spread across the leaves of croton. Provide four hours of direct sunlight daily and pinch back frequently. Use leaves in arrangements after splitting the stem ends and standing them in water overnight.

FITTONIA, SILVER-NERVED. Creeping plants with delicate silver-white or red markings along their leaf veins, fittonias are excellent pot plants for low-light locations.

ORCHID, VANDA. Clusters of speckled and netted flower pinwheels appear two or three times a year on long spikes growing among the leathery strap-shaped leaves of vanda orchids. Provide bright indirect or filtered sunlight, and keep pots on a tray of moist pebbles to assure high humidity. Cut orchids when they are fully open. Place stems in water vials or tape a piece of moistened cotton to each cut stem, then refrigerate until used. Check the water level in arrangements daily and keep them in cool locations. Place corsages in the refrigerator when they are not being worn.

PAINTED TONGUE. Shaped like petunias, the velvety flower trumpets of painted tongue are delicately veined in contrasting colors. Fully open flowers last three to five days in arrangements if they first stand overnight in water that reaches up to the flowers.

PANSY. Available in many colors, pansies are ideal for pots and window boxes in sunny locations. To arrange, choose fully open flowers, pulling rather than cutting them off. Submerge in cold water until the petals are crisp, then stand stems overnight in water. Thus conditioned, pansies last up to a week. Pansies dry in one to one and one half days in silica gel but then should be sprayed with hair spray or plastic fixative to protect them from humidity.

PRAYER PLANT. The leaves of the prayer plant, which fold vertically in the dark, seem painted with fishbone patterns. Provide bright indirect sunlight.

SWEDISH IVY. The thick scalloped leaves of various species of Swedish ivy are edged in white, lined with silver veins, or tinged purple on their undersides. Provide curtain-filtered sunlight and pinch back often to promote branching.

WINTER CREEPER. Several varieties of winter creeper have white or gold edgings along the shrub's shiny green oval leaves. Although it grows four feet tall, winter creeper is easily shaped by pruning and can be grown in a tub in sunlight or light shade. Small plants can be grown indoors in pots if they are given bright indirect light and cool temperatures ranging from 40° at night up to 65° by day.

Conditioning plant materials, page 58; drying plant materials, page 67.

Appendix

Characteristics of 171 plant materials

Listed below for quick reference are the plants, cut flowers and plant materials illustrated in Chapter 5.

Plant	Green	Yellow	Orange	Red	Purple	Blue	White	Multicolor	Bold	Lacy	Rounded	Arching	Spiky	Sculptural	Rough	Feathery	Waxy	Striped	Spotted	Variegated	Under 1 foot	1 to 2 feet	2 to 3 feet	Over 3 feet
AFRICAN VIOLET *Saintpaulia ionantha*			•	•	•	•	•													•	•			
AGERATUM *Ageratum houstonianum*				•	•	•							•							•	•	•		
ALOE, TIGER *Aloe variegata*							•							•			•			•	•			
AMARYLLIS *Hippeastrum* hybrid			•	•			•	•											•	•	•			
APPLE *Malus* varieties		•		•					•							•				•		•		
ASPARAGUS FERN, FOXTAIL *Asparagus myersii*	•															•					•			
ASTER *Aster* species and hybrids				•	•	•	•													•	•	•	•	•
ASTILBE *Astilbe arendsii*				•			•									•							•	
BABIES'-BREATH *Gypsophila paniculata*				•			•			•														•
BEGONIA, IRON CROSS *Begonia masoniana*	•						•								•				•	•				
BEGONIA, RIEGER *Begonia elatior*		•	•	•			•				•										•			
BEGONIA TREEBINE *Cissus discolor*							•													•				
BELLS-OF-IRELAND *Moluccella laevis*	•												•									•		
BIRD-OF-PARADISE *Strelitzia reginae*								•	•															•
BLACK-EYED-SUSAN VINE *Thunbergia alata*		•	•				•																•	•
BLUE LACE FLOWER *Trachymene caerulea*					•	•																•		
BLUE MARGUERITE *Felicia amelloides*					•															•				
BUGBANE, KAMCHATKA *Cimicifuga simplex*					•						•					•						•		
BURRO'S TAIL *Sedum morganianum*	•										•	•								•				
BUTTERFLY WEED *Asclepias tuberosa*			•																	•				
BUTTERNUT *Juglans cinerea*																				•				
CACTUS, BUNNY EARS *Opuntia microdasys*	•												•	•										•
CACTUS, GOLDEN BARREL *Echinocactus grusonii*	•										•			•									•	
CACTUS, GOLDEN EASTER LILY *Lobivia aurea*	•										•			•						•				
CACTUS, OLD-MAN *Cephalocereus senilis*					•									•						•				
CACTUS, RATTAIL *Aporocactus flagelliformis*	•											•		•									•	
CALADIUM *Caladium hortulanum*			•				•	•	•										•	•	•	•		
CALENDULA *Calendula officinalis*		•	•				•		•											•				
CALICO HEARTS *Adromischus maculatus*	•								•						•					•				
CALLA LILY *Zantedeschia* species		•	•	•			•	•						•							•	•	•	
CAMELLIA, COMMON *Camellia japonica*				•			•	•			•						•							•
CARNATION *Dianthus caryophyllus*		•	•	•			•	•											•		•	•		
CENTURY PLANT, QUEEN VICTORIA *Agave victoriae-reginae*	•												•	•						•				
CHESTNUT, CHINESE *Castanea mollissima*															•					•				
CHINESE LANTERN PLANT *Physalis alkekengi*			•																	•				
CHRISTMAS CACTUS *Schlumbergera-Zygocactus* hybrid			•	•		•						•		•						•				
CHRISTMAS HEATH *Erica canaliculata*			•							•										•				
CHRYSANTHEMUM, HARDY *Chrysanthemum morifolium*		•	•	•	•		•		•											•	•	•	•	
CINERARIA *Senecio cruentus*				•	•	•	•													•		•		
COCKSCOMB *Celosia argentea cristata*		•	•	•				•							•					•	•	•	•	•
COLEUS *Coleus blumei*								•										•	•	•	•			
COREOPSIS *Coreopsis* species		•	•	•																•	•	•		
CORNFLOWER *Centaurea cyanus*				•	•	•	•													•	•	•	•	
COW PARSNIP *Heracleum maximum*							•			•														•
CROCUS *Crocus* hybrids		•		•	•	•	•											•		•				
CROTON *Codiaeum variegatum*							•	•												•				•
CUSHION SPURGE *Euphorbia epithymoides*	•	•																		•				
CYCLAMEN *Cyclamen persicum*				•	•		•													•	•	•		
DAFFODIL *Narcissus* species		•	•	•			•	•												•	•	•		
DAY LILY *Hemerocallis* hybrids		•	•	•			•													•	•	•	•	•

Plant	COLOR								SHAPE						TEXTURE			PATTERN			HEIGHT OR LENGTH			
	Green	Yellow	Orange	Red	Purple	Blue	White	Multicolor	Bold	Lacy	Rounded	Arching	Spiky	Sculptural	Rough	Feathery	Waxy	Striped	Spotted	Variegated	Under 1 foot	1 to 2 feet	2 to 3 feet	Over 3 feet
DELPHINIUM, CANDLE *Delphinium elatum* hybrids				●	●	●						●												●
DIEFFENBACHIA, RUDOLF ROEHRS *Dieffenbachia picta*	●							●												●				●
DOGWOOD, FLOWERING *Cornus florida*			●				●																	●
DRACAENA, FLORIDA BEAUTY *Dracaena godseffiana*								●										●					●	
DRACAENA, MASSANGE'S *Dracaena fragrans massangeana*								●				●						●						●
DYCKIA *Dyckia fosterana*			●	●									●										●	
EARTH STAR *Cryptanthus bivittatus*								●					●							●				
ELEPHANT-FOOT TREE *Beaucarnea recurvata*	●											●		●										●
FALSE ARALIA *Dizygotheca elegantissima*	●									●														●
FATSIA, JAPANESE *Fatsia japonica*	●									●														●
FERN, BIRD'S-NEST *Asplenium nidus*	●											●										●	●	●
FERN, BOSTON *Nephrolepis exaltata bostoniensis*	●									●		●										●	●	●
FERN, BUTTON *Pellaea rotundifolia*	●																					●		
FERN, FAN MAIDENHAIR *Adiantum tenerum wrightii*	●									●												●		
FERN, FIJI DAVALLIA *Davallia fejeensis*	●									●												●		
FERN, FLUFFY RUFFLES *Nephrolepis exaltata*	●															●						●		
FERN, SPEAR-LEAVED *Doryopteris pedata palmata*	●									●												●		
FERN, STAGHORN *Platycerium bifurcatum*	●													●									●	
FIRE THORN, LALAND *Pyracantha coccinea lalandei*			●	●																				●
FITTONIA, SILVER-NERVED *Fittonia argyroneura*	●																		●	●				
FLOWERING TOBACCO *Nicotiana alata grandiflora*	●	●	●	●	●		●														●	●		
FORSYTHIA, BORDER *Forsythia intermedia*		●									●													●
FOXGLOVE, COMMON *Digitalis purpurea*		●	●	●	●		●						●											●
FRECKLE FACE *Hypoestes phyllostachya*								●											●		●	●		
GARDENIA *Gardenia jasminoides veitchii*							●															●	●	
GASTERIA, OXTONGUE *Gasteria verrucosa*	●												●					●			●			
GERANIUM, COMMON *Pelargonium hortorum*			●	●	●		●				●										●	●	●	
GLADIOLUS *Gladiolus* hybrids and species		●	●	●	●	●	●	●					●									●	●	●
GLOBE THISTLE *Echinops* species					●						●													●
GLOXINIA *Sinningia speciosa*			●	●	●	●	●												●	●	●			
GOLD-DUST TREE *Aucuba japonica variegata*								●											●				●	
GOLDENROD *Solidago* species and hybrids		●														●							●	●
GOURD *Gourd* species	●	●	●				●	●			●			●			●				●	●	●	●
GRAPE HYACINTH *Muscari armeniacum*				●	●	●															●			
GRASS, CLOUD *Agrostis nebulosa*						●				●											●			
GRASS, PAMPAS *Cortaderia selloana*			●				●									●								●
GRASS, RABBIT-TAIL *Lagurus ovatus*																●						●		
GRASS, RUBY *Rhynchelytrum repens*			●											●		●								●
GRASS, SQUIRRELTAIL *Hordeum jubatum*																●					●	●	●	
HAWORTHIA, PEARLY *Haworthia margaritifera*	●												●	●							●			
HOLLY, ENGLISH *Ilex aquifolium*				●																				●
HYACINTH *Hyacinthus* species		●		●	●	●							●								●			
HYDRANGEA, COMMON BIGLEAF *Hydrangea macrophylla*				●	●	●	●				●													●
IMPATIENS *Impatiens wallerana*			●	●	●		●	●													●	●		
INDOOR OAK *Nicodemia diversifolia*	●																					●		
IRIS *Iris* hybrids and species	●	●	●	●	●	●	●	●													●	●	●	●
JADE PLANT *Crassula argentea*	●													●								●	●	
JASMINE, POET'S *Jasminum officinale grandiflorum*							●			●														●
KOHLERIA *Kohleria amabilis*								●											●		●	●	●	
LAVENDER, TRUE *Lavandula officinalis*				●									●									●	●	

Plant	Green	Yellow	Orange	Red	Purple	Blue	White	Multicolor	Bold	Lacy	Rounded	Arching	Spiky	Sculptural	Rough	Feathery	Waxy	Striped	Spotted	Variegated	Under 1 foot	1 to 2 feet	2 to 3 feet	Over 3 feet
LILAC, COMMON *Syringa vulgaris*		●		●	●	●	●																	●
LILY *Lilium* species and hybrids		●	●	●	●		●	●										●				●	●	●
LILY, EASTER *Lilium longiflorum*							●															●	●	
LILY OF THE VALLEY *Convallaria majalis*							●														●			
MAGNOLIA, SOUTHERN *Magnolia grandiflora*							●										●				●	●		
MARIGOLD *Tagetes* species		●	●					●													●	●	●	
MIGNONETTE *Reseda odorata*		●		●										●						●				
MILK-STRIPED EUPHORBIA *Euphorbia lactea*	●												●	●			●					●		
MONKEY FLOWER *Mimulus* hybrids		●		●			●											●			●			
MONSTERA *Monstera deliciosa*	●									●				●										●
MOONSTONES *Pachyphytum oviferum*	●													●						●				
MOSES-IN-THE-CRADLE, VARIEGATED *Rhoeo spathacea vittata*							●										●			●	●			
NASTURTIUM, COMMON *Tropaeolum majus*		●	●	●			●													●	●	●		
NATAL PLUM *Carissa grandiflora*							●													●				
NIDULARIUM *Nidularium regelioides*							●				●									●				
NORFOLK ISLAND PINE *Araucaria heterophylla*	●												●											●
ORANGE, CALAMONDIN *Citrus mitis*		●					●													●				
ORCHID, CATTLEYA *Cattleya* hybrids and species	●	●	●	●	●	●	●	●	●												●	●		
ORCHID, PAPHIOPEDILUM *Paphiopedilum bellatulum*							●												●	●				
ORCHID, VANDA *Vanda rothschildiana*	●	●	●	●	●	●	●												●	●			●	●
ORNAMENTAL CABBAGE *Brassica oleracea capitata*							●				●									●				
PAINTED TONGUE *Salpiglossis sinuata*		●		●	●	●	●												●		●	●		
PALM, CHINESE FAN *Livistona chinensis*	●											●												●
PALM, SAGO *Cycas revoluta*	●											●											●	
PALM, TUFTED FISHTAIL *Caryota mitis*	●											●		●										●
PANAMIGA *Pilea involucrata*			●													●				●				
PANDA PLANT *Kalanchoe tomentosa*	●																			●				
PANSY *Viola* species							●												●	●				
PEONY, CHINESE *Paeonia lactiflora*		●		●	●		●				●													●
PEPEROMIA, WATERMELON *Peperomia sandersii*							●											●		●				
PEPPER PLANT *Capsicum annuum conoides*							●										●			●				
PETUNIA *Petunia* hybrids		●	●	●	●	●	●	●												●	●	●		
PHILODENDRON, HEART-LEAVED *Philodendron oxycardium*	●													●										●
PHILODENDRON, SADDLE-LEAVED *Philodendron selloum*	●								●															●
PHILODENDRON, WENDLAND'S *Philodendron wendlandii*	●								●											●				
PINE, RED *Pinus resinosa*													●							●				●
PINE, TANYOSHO *Pinus densiflora umbraculifera*	●																							●
PINK PLUME POPPY *Macleaya cordata*										●														●
PITTOSPORUM, JAPANESE *Pittosporum tobira*	●																●							●
POCKETBOOK FLOWER *Calceolaria herbeohybrida*		●		●			●												●	●	●			
PODOCARPUS, CHINESE *Podocarpus macrophyllus maki*	●													●										●
PRAYER PLANT *Maranta leuconeura*	●						●												●	●				
PRIVET, WAX-LEAVED *Ligustrum japonicum*	●																●							●
PURPLE HEART *Setcreasea purpurea*					●															●				
ROSE Hybrid tea varieties	●	●	●	●	●		●	●												●			●	
RUBBER TREE, BROAD-LEAVED INDIA *Ficus elastica decora*	●																●							●
SANSEVIERIA *Sansevieria trifasciata*	●												●				●			●	●	●	●	
SCHEFFLERA *Brassaia actinophylla*	●										●													●
SEA HOLLY, OLIVER *Eryngium oliverianum*					●	●								●										●
SEA LAVENDER, WIDE-LEAVED *Limonium latifolium*					●	●		●												●				

Plant	Green	Yellow	Orange	Red	Purple	Blue	White	Multicolor	Bold	Lacy	Rounded	Arching	Spiky	Sculptural	Rough	Feathery	Waxy	Striped	Spotted	Variegated	Under 1 foot	1 to 2 feet	2 to 3 feet	Over 3 feet
SEERSUCKER PLANT *Geogenanthus undatus*								●									●			●				
SHASTA DAISY *Chrysanthemum maximum*							●				●											●	●	
SNAPDRAGON *Antirrhinum majus*		●	●	●	●		●	●					●								●	●	●	●
SPIDER PLANT, COMMON *Chlorophytum comosum vittatum*	●							●									●			●	●			
SPIRAL FLAG *Costus sanguineus*								●									●						●	
STRAWFLOWER *Helichrysum bracteatum*		●	●	●	●		●				●												●	
STREPTOSOLEN, ORANGE *Streptosolen jamesonii*			●																				●	
STRIPED INCH PLANT *Callisia elegans*								●									●						●	
SUNFLOWER, COMMON *Helianthus annuus*	●								●		●													●
SWEDISH IVY, WHITE-EDGED *Plectranthus coleoides marginatus*								●											●	●				
TAILFLOWER *Anthurium andreanum*			●			●										●							●	
THERMOPSIS, CAROLINA *Thermopsis caroliniana*	●												●											●
TIGERFLOWER *Tigridia pavonia*								●											●		●	●		
TITHONIA *Tithonia rotundifolia*			●	●							●													●
TULIP *Tulipa* hybrids		●	●	●	●		●	●									●			●	●	●	●	
URN PLANT *Aechmea fasciata*								●						●			●						●	
WANDERING JEW, FOUR-COLORED *Zebrina pendula quadricolor*								●									●							●
WAX PLANT *Hoya carnosa*			●					●								●			●				●	
WINTER CREEPER, EMERALD 'N GOLD *Euonymus fortunei*								●											●					●
YARROW, FERN-LEAVED *Achillea filipendulina*		●		●		●																	●	●
ZEBRA PLANT *Aphelandra squarrosa*								●									●					●		

Picture credits

Bibliography

Ackerman, Isabel T., Housekeeper, Rose Batterham, and Thacher, Emma E., *Harmony in Flower Design.* Dodd, Mead & Co., 1939.

Arms, John Taylor, and Noyes, Dorothy, *Design in Flower Arrangement.* Macmillan Publishing Co., Inc., 1937.

Ascher, Amalie Adler, *The Complete Flower Arranger.* Simon & Schuster, Inc., 1974.

Ballard, Ernesta Drinker, *The Art of Training Plants.* Harper & Row, 1974.

Ballard, Ernesta Drinker, *Garden in Your House,* revised edition. Harper & Row Publishers, Inc., 1971.

Baumgardt, John Philip, *Hanging Plants for Home, Terrace, and Garden.* Simon & Schuster, Inc., 1972.

Bear, Elizabeth, *Better Flower Arrangements for Home and Exhibition.* Laurel Publishing Corp., 1953.

Berrall, Julia S., *A History of Flower Arrangement.* The Viking Press, 1968.

Brooklyn Botanic Garden, *Bonsai for Indoors.* BBG, 1976.

Brooks, Myra J., *Flower Arrangement Workbook 1.* M. Barrows & Co., 1953.

Bugbee, Audrey Steiner, *How to Dry Flowers the Easy Way.* Houghton Mifflin Co., 1975.

Chittenden, Fred J., ed., *The Royal Horticultural Society Dictionary of Gardening,* 2nd ed. Clarendon Press, 1974.

Condon, Geneal, *The Complete Book of Flower Preservation.* Prentice-Hall, Inc., 1970.

Cruso, Thalassa, *Making Things Grow.* Alfred A. Knopf, Inc., 1976.

Eichler, Lillian, *The Customs of Mankind.* Norwood Editions, 1937.

Elbert, Virginie F. and George A., *The House Plant Decorating Book.* E. P. Dutton and Co., Inc., 1977.

Ferrari, P. Giovanni Battista, *Flora—Ouero Cultura di Fiori.* Rome, 1638.

Fitch, Charles Marden, *The Complete Book of Houseplants.* Hawthorn Books, Inc., 1972.

Fort, Marie Johnson, *Flower Arrangements for All Occasions.* Rinehart & Co., 1952.

Graf, Alfred Byrd, *Exotic Plant Manual,* 4th ed. Roehrs Co., Inc., 1974.

Harshbarger, Gretchen Fitch, *McCall's Gardening Book.* Simon & Schuster, Inc., 1968.

Hillier, Florence Bell, *Basic Guide to Flower Arranging.* McGraw-Hill Book Co., 1974.

Hunter, Sam, *Modern French Painting 1855-1956.* Dell Publishing Co., Inc., 1956.

Ikenobo, Senei, *Best of Ikebana—Ikenobo School.* Shufunotomo Co., Ltd., Tokyo, 1962.

Johns, Leslie, *Plants in Tubs, Pots, Boxes and Baskets.* Van Nostrand Reinhold Co., 1974.

Karel, Leonard, *Dried Flowers From Antiquity to the Present.* The Scarecrow Press, Inc., 1973.

Kasperski, Victoria R., *How to Make Cut Flowers Last.* M. Barrows and Co., Inc., 1956.

Klamkin, Marian, *Flower Arranging for Period Decoration.* Funk & Wagnalls, 1968.

Kramer, Jack, *Beyond the House Plant: How to Build, Plant and Care for a Garden in Limited Space.* Ballantine Books, Inc., 1976.

Kramer, Jack, *Container Gardening Indoors and Out.* Doubleday & Co., Inc., 1971.

Kramer, Jack, *Ferns and Palms for Interior Decoration.* Charles Scribner's Sons, 1972.

Kramer, Jack, *Hanging Gardens.* Charles Scribner's Sons, 1971.

Kramer, Jack, and Adkinson, Andrew R., *How to Use Houseplants Indoors for Beauty and Decoration.* Doubleday & Co., Inc., 1974.

Lipman, Jean, and Winchester, Alice, *The Flowering of American Folk Art (1776-1876)*. The Viking Press, Inc., 1974.

Lipman, Jean, and Winchester, Alice, *Primitive Painters in America 1750-1950*. Dodd, Mead & Co., 1950.

Marcus, Margaret Fairbanks, *Period Flower Arrangement*. M. Barrows & Co., Inc., 1952.

McDonald, Elvin, *Hanging Gardens*. Grosset & Dunlap Inc., 1976.

Metropolitan Museum of Art in New York, *Flowers: The Flower Piece in European Painting*. Harper & Brothers Publishers, 1949.

Mitchell, Peter, *Great Flower Painters*. The Overlook Press, 1973.

Nakajima, Tameji, *The Art of the Chrysanthemum*. Harper & Row Publishers, Inc., 1965.

Nehrling, Arno and Irene, *Gardening, Forcing, Conditioning and Drying for Flower Arrangements*. Hearthside Press, Inc., 1958.

Nichols, Beverley, *The Art of Flower Arrangement*. The Viking Press, 1967.

Ohara, Houn, *Best of Ikebana—Ohara School*. Shufunotomo Co., Ltd., Tokyo, 1962.

Ortho Books, *Container and Hanging Gardens*. Chevron Chemical Co., 1975.

Ortho Books, *The Facts of Light about Indoor Gardening*. Chevron Chemical Co., 1975.

Pulbrook, Susan, and Gould, Rosamund, *The Gracious Art of Flower Arrangement*. Doubleday & Co., Inc., 1968.

Richie, Donald, ed., *The Masters' Book of Ikebana*. Bijutsu Shuppan-sha, Tokyo, 1966.

Rockwell, F. F., and Grayson, Esther C., *The New Complete Book of Flower Arrangement*. Doubleday & Co., Inc., 1960.

Rogers, Matilda, *Flower Arrangements Anyone Can Do*. Dodd, Mead & Co., 1954.

Safford, Carleton L., and Bishop, Robert, *America's Quilts and Coverlets*. Weathervane Books, a division of Barre Publishing Co., Inc., 1974.

Shinno, Tat, *Flower Arranging by Tat*. Fashion Press, 1961.

Shinohara, Takeshi, *Kikuzukuri Nyumon*. Nippon Bungei-sha, Tokyo, 1977.

Skelsey, Alice, and Mooney, Cecile, *Every Room a Garden*.

Workman Publishing Co., Inc., 1976.

Society of American Florists, *Care and Handling of Flowers and Plants*. S.A.F., 1976.

Spry, Constance, *The Art of Arranging Flowers*. Thomas Y. Crowell, 1953.

Spry, Constance, *Flower Decoration*. G. P. Putnam's Sons, 1933.

Squires, Mabel, *The Art of Drying Plants and Flowers*. Bonanza Books, 1958.

Staff of the L. H. Bailey Hortorium, Cornell University, *Hortus Third: A Dictionary of Plants Cultivated in the United States and Canada*. Macmillan Publishing Co., Inc., 1976.

Sunset Editors, *Gardening in Containers*, revised edition. Lane Publishing Co., 1967.

Sunset Editors, *Hanging Gardens*. Lane Publishing Co., 1974.

Teshigawara, Kasumi, *Space and Color in Japanese Flower Arrangement*. Kodansha International Ltd., Tokyo, 1965.

Teuscher, Henry, *Window-Box Gardening*. Macmillan Publishing Co., 1956.

Vance, Georgia S., *The Decorative Art of Dried Flower Arrangement*. Doubleday & Co., Inc., 1972.

Wagner, Leopold, *Manners, Customs, and Observances*. Gale Research Co., 1968.

Wallach, Carla, *Gardening in the City: Backyards, Balconies, Terraces and Penthouses*. Harcourt, Brace, Jovanovich, Inc., 1976.

Wallach, Carla, *Interior Decorating with Plants*. Macmillan Publishing Co., Inc., 1976.

Walsh, William S., *Curiosities of Popular Custom*. J. B. Lippincott Company, 1875.

Westland, Pamela, and Critchley, Paula, *The Art of Dried and Pressed Flowers*. Crown Publishers, Inc., 1974.

Wheeler, Esther, and Lasker, Anabel C., *The Complete Book of Flowers and Plants for Interior Decoration*, revised edition. Hearthside Press, Inc., 1969.

Wright, Michael, and Brown, Dennis, eds., *The Complete Indoor Gardener*. Random House, Inc., 1975.

Wyman, Donald, *Wyman's Gardening Encyclopedia*. Macmillan Publishing Co., Inc., 1971.

Yang, Linda, *The Terrace Gardener's Handbook*. Doubleday & Co., Inc., 1975.

Acknowledgments

The index for this book was prepared by Anita R. Beckerman. For their help in the preparation of this book, the editors wish to thank the following: Ernesta Drinker Ballard, Pennsylvania Horticultural Society, Philadelphia, Pa.; Pat Braun, Madderlake, New York City; Dr. Gerald Carlson, Agricultural Research Service, U.S. Department of Agriculture, Beltsville, Md.; Patricia Chandler, New Orleans, La.; Mrs. William Connolly, Pelham, N.Y.; Mrs. K. K. Dastur, Pelham, N.Y.; Loral Dean, Atlanta, Ga.; Phyllis Elliott, The Plant Store, Alexandria, Va.; Enid Farmer, Lexington, Mass.; Galper Baldon Associates, Venice, Calif.; Rosemary Gillett, Winter Park, Fla.; Aiko Hideshima, Tokyo, Japan; Irene Jones, New York City; Jean Keith, Alexandria, Va.; Mr. and Mrs. Arthur Korf, Phoenix, Ariz.; Terry Lewis, John Tilton Assoc., Inc., Chicago, Ill.; Dr. Conrad Link, Department of Horticulture, University of Maryland, College Park, Md.; Daisy Logan, The Plant Store, Alexandria, Va.; Barbara Ludvigsen, Decoration Day, Ltd., Larchmont, N.Y.; Nancy Marshall, Alexandria, Va.; Dr. Bruce McAlpin, New York Botanical Garden, New York City; Mr. and Mrs. O. B. McEwan, Orlando, Fla.; Mrs. Robert Moderelli, Pelham, N.Y.; Bruce Nash, Alexandria Floral Co., Alexandria, Va.; Carolyn Noble, Pelham, N.Y.; J. Liddon Pennock Jr., Meadowbrook Farm Greenhouse, Meadowbrook, Pa.; Robert Pierce, St. Louis, Mo.; Pearl April Richlin, Sherman Oaks, Calif.; The River Port Garden Club, Alexandria, Va.; the staff of Robert E. Lee's Boyhood Home, Alexandria, Va.; Jacqueline Schmeal, Houston, Tex.; Vicki Shaper, Roslyn, Long Island, N.Y.; Bill Sprague, Annandale, Va.; Dr. William Louis Stern, Division of Agricultural and Life Sciences, University of Maryland, College Park, Md.; Mr. and Mrs. Brooke E. Supplee, New York City; Mrs. Hale H. Taylor, McLean, Va.; Michael Taylor, San Francisco, Calif.; John Tilton, John Tilton Assoc., Inc., Chicago, Ill.; Mutsuo Tomita, Ohara Center of New York, New York City; Susan Tuttle, Alexandria, Va.; Nijole Valaitis, Irvington-on-Hudson, N.Y.; John S. Voloudakis, Scottsdale, Ariz.; Robert A. Wearne, Extension Service, U.S. Department of Agriculture, Washington, D.C.

Index

Numerals in italics indicate an illustration of the subject mentioned.

PRINTED IN U.S.A.